Robert Disch, MA
Rose Dobrof, DSW
Harry R. Moody, PhD
Editors

Dignity and Old Age

Dignity and Old Age has been co-published simultaneously as *Journal of Gerontological Social Work*, Volume 29, Numbers 2/3 1998.

Pre-publication
REVIEWS,
COMMENTARIES,
EVALUATIONS . . .

"**C**HALLENGES US TO UPHOLD THE RIGHT TO AGE WITH DIGNITY, which is embedded in the heart and soul of every man and woman. Aging with dignity may mean different things to people of different age, gender, race or financial status; however, our common humanity impels us to protect this right to age with dignity for ourselves, and for each other."

"**M**any people talk about dignity. THIS BOOK DOES SOMETHING ABOUT IT."

H. James Towey
President
Commission on Aging with Dignity
Tallahassee, FL

Robert D. Butler, MD
Director
International Longevity Center
Mt. Sinai Medical Center
New York, NY

Dignity and Old Age

Dignity and Old Age has been co-published simultaneously as *Journal of Gerontological Social Work*, Volume 29, Numbers 2/3 1998.

The *Journal of Gerontological Social Work* Monographs/"Separates"

Gerontological Social Work Practice in Long-Term Care,
  edited by George S. Getzel and M. Joanna Mellor

A Healthy Old Age: A Sourcebook for Health Promotion with Older Adults,
  edited by Stephanie FallCreek and Molly K. Mettler

The Uses of Reminiscence: New Ways of Working with Older Adults,
  edited by Marc Kaminsky

Gerontological Social Work in Home Health Care, edited by Rose Dobrof

Gerontological Social Work Practice in the Community,
  edited by George S. Getzel and M. Joanna Mellor

Social Work and Alzheimer's Disease, edited by Rose Dobrof

Ethnicity and Gerontological Social Work, edited by Rose Dobrof

*Gerontological Social Work Practice with Families: A Guide to Practice Issues
  and Service Delivery*, edited by Rose Dobrof

Gerontological Social Work: International Perspectives,
  edited by Merl C. Hokenstad, Jr. and Katherine A. Kendall

*Twenty-Five Years of the Life Review: Theoretical and Practical
  Considerations*, edited by Robert Disch

Health Care of the Aged: Needs, Policies, and Services,
  edited by Abraham Monk

Vision and Aging: Issues in Social Work Practice, edited by Nancy D. Weber

Geriatric Social Work Education, edited by M. Joanna Mellor
  and Renee Solomon

*New Developments in Home Care Services for the Elderly: Innovations
  in Policy, Program, and Practice*, edited by Lenard W. Kaye

Special Aging Populations and Systems Linkages, edited by M. Joanna Mellor

*Social Work Response to the White House Conference on Aging: From Issues
  to Actions*, edited by Constance Corley Saltz

*Intergenerational Approaches in Aging: Implications for Education, Policy
  and Practice*, edited by Kevin Brabazon and Robert Disch

Dignity and Old Age, edited by Rose Dobrof and Harry R. Moody

These books were published simultaneously as special thematic issues of the *Journal of Gerontological Social Work* and are available bound separately. Visit Haworth's website at http://www.haworthpressinc.com to search our online catalog for complete tables of contents and ordering information for these and other publications. Or call 1-800-HAWORTH (outside US/Canada: 607-722-5857), Fax: 1-800-895-0582 (outside US/Canada: 607-771-0012), or e-mail getinfo@ haworthpressinc.com

Dignity and Old Age

Robert Disch, MA
Rose Dobrof, DSW
Harry R. Moody, PhD
Editors

Dignity and Old Age has been co-published simultaneously as *Journal of Gerontological Social Work*, Volume 29, Numbers 2/3 1998.

The Haworth Press, Inc.
New York • London

Dignity and old age /

Dignity and Old Age has been co-published simultaneously as *Journal of Gerontological Social Work™*, Volume 29, Numbers 2/3 1998.

The Haworth Press, Inc., 10 Alice Street, Binghamton, NY 13904-1580 USA

Cover design by Thomas J. Mayshock Jr.

Library of Congress Cataloging-in-Publication Data

Dignity and old age / Robert Disch, Rose Dobrof, Harry R. Moody, editors.
     p. cm.
     Co-published simultaneously as Journal of Gerontological Social Work, vol. 29, numbers 2/3 1998.
     Includes bibliographical references and index.
     ISBN 0-7890-0534-4 (alk. paper)
     1. Social work with the aged. 2. Aged–Services for. 3. Dignity. 4. Quality of life. I. Disch, Robert. II. Dobrof, Rose. III. Moody, Harry R.
HV1451.D52 1998
362.6–dc21   98-17892
                                                         CIP

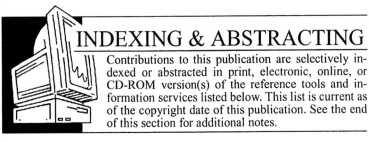

INDEXING & ABSTRACTING

Contributions to this publication are selectively indexed or abstracted in print, electronic, online, or CD-ROM version(s) of the reference tools and information services listed below. This list is current as of the copyright date of this publication. See the end of this section for additional notes.

- *Abstracts in Social Gerontology: Current Literature on Aging*, National Council on the Aging, Library, 409 Third Street SW, 2nd Floor, Washington, DC 20024

- *Academic Abstracts/CD-ROM*, EBSCO Publishing Editorial Department, P.O. Box 590, Ipswich, MA 01938-0590

- *Academic Search: data base of 2,000 selected academic serials, updated monthly*, EBSCO Publishing, 83 Pine Street, Peabody, MA 01960

- *AgeInfo CD-Rom*, Centre for Policy on Ageing, 25-31 Ironmonger Row, London EC1V 3QP, England

- *AgeLine Database*, American Association of Retired Persons, 601 E Street, NW, Washington, DC 20049

- *Alzheimer's Disease Education & Referral Center (ADEAR)*, Combined Health Information Database (CHID), P.O. Box 8250, Silver Spring, MD 20907-8250

- *Applied Social Sciences Index & Abstracts (ASSIA) (Online: ASSI via Data-Star) (CDRom: ASSIA Plus)*, Bowker-Saur Limited, Maypole House, Maypole Road, East Grinstead, West Sussex RH19 1HH, England

- *Behavioral Medicine Abstracts*, University of Washington, Department of Social Work & Speech & Hearing Sciences, Box 354900, Seattle, WA 98195

- *Biosciences Information Service of Biological Abstracts (BIOSIS)*, Biosciences Information Service, 2100 Arch Street, Philadelphia, PA 19103-1399

(continued)

- ***Brown University Geriatric Research Application Digest
  "Abstracts Section,"*** Brown University, Center for
  Gerontology & Health Care Research, c/o Box G-B 235,
  Providence, RI 02912

- ***caredata CD: the social and community care database***,
  National Institute for Social Work, 5 Tavistock Place,
  London WC1H 9SS, England

- ***CINAHL (Cumulative Index to Nursing & Allied Health
  Literature), in print, also on CD-ROM from CD PLUS,
  EBSCO, and SilverPlatter, and online from CDP Online
  (formerly BRS), Data-Star, and PaperChase. (Support
  materials include Subject Heading List, Database Search
  Guide, and instructional video.)***, CINAHL Information
  Systems, P.O. Box 871/1509 Wilson Terrace, Glendale, CA
  91209-0871

- ***CNPIEC Reference Guide: Chinese National Directory
  of Foreign Periodicals***, P.O. Box 88, Beijing, People's
  Republic of China

- ***Criminal Justice Abstracts***, Willow Tree Press, 15 Washington
  Street, 4th Floor, Newark, NJ 07102

- ***Current Contents. . . . see: Institute for Scientific Information***

- ***Expanded Academic Index***, Information Access Company,
  362 Lakeside Drive, Forest City, CA 94404

- ***Family Studies Database (online and CD/ROM)***, National
  Information Services Corporation, 306 East Baltimore Pike,
  2nd Floor, Media, PA 19063

- ***Family Violence & Sexual Assault Bulletin***, Family Violence &
  Sexual Assault Institute, 1121 E South East Loop #323,
  Suite 130, Tyler, TX 75701

- ***Gay & Lesbian Abstracts***, National Information Services
  Corporation, 306 East Baltimore Pike, Second Floor, Media,
  PA 19063

- ***Human Resources Abstracts (HRA)***, Sage Publications, Inc.,
  2455 Teller Road, Newbury Park, CA 91320

(continued)

- *IBZ International Bibliography of Periodical Literature*, Zeller Verlag GmbH & Co., P.O.B. 1949, D-49009 Osnabruck, Germany

- *Index to Periodical Articles Related to Law*, University of Texas, 727 East 26th Street, Austin, TX 78705

- *Institute for Scientific Information*, 3501 Market Street, Philadelphia, PA 19104-3302 (USA). Coverage in:
  a) Research Alert (current awareness service)
  b) Social SciSearch (magnetic tape)
  c) Current Contents/Social & Behavioral Sciences (weekly current awareness service)

- *MasterFILE: updated database from EBSCO Publishing*, EBSCO Publishing, 83 Pine Street, Peabody, MA 01960

- *National Clearinghouse for Primary Care Information (NCPCI)*, 2070 Chain Bridge Road, Suite 450, Vienna, VA 22182-2536

- *New Literature on Old Age*, Centre for Policy on Ageing, 25-31 Ironmonger Row, London EC1V 3QP, England

- *Periodical Abstracts, Research I (general & basic reference indexing & abstracting data-base from University Microfilms International (UMI), 300 North Zeeb Road, P.O. Box 1346, Ann Arbor, MI 48106-1346)*, UMI Data Courier, P.O. Box 32770, Louisville, KY 40232-2770

- *Periodical Abstracts, Research II (broad coverage indexing & abstracting data-base from University Microfilms International (UMI), 300 North Zeeb Road, P.O. Box 1346, Ann Arbor, MI 48106-1346)*, UMI Data Courier, P.O. Box 32770, Louisville, KY 40232-2770

- *Psychological Abstracts (PsycINFO)*, American Psychological Association, P.O. Box 91600, Washington, DC 20090-1600

- *Social Planning/Policy & Development Abstracts (SOPODA)*, Sociological Abstracts, Inc., P.O. Box 22206, San Diego, CA 92192-0206

- *Social Science Citation Index. . . . see: Institute for Scientific Information*

(continued)

- *Social Science Source: coverage of 400 journals in the social sciences area; updated monthly,* EBSCO Publishing, P.O. Box 2250, Peabody, MA 01960-7250

- *Social Sciences Index (from Volume 1 & continuing),* The H. W. Wilson Company, 950 University Avenue, Bronx, NY 10452

- *Social Work Abstracts,* National Association of Social Workers, 750 First Street NW, 8th Floor, Washington, DC 20002

- *Sociological Abstracts (SA),* Sociological Abstracts, Inc., P.O. Box 22206, San Diego, CA 92192-0206

SPECIAL BIBLIOGRAPHIC NOTES

related to special journal issues (separates)
and indexing/abstracting

☐ indexing/abstracting services in this list will also cover material in any "separate" that is co-published simultaneously with Haworth's special thematic journal issue or DocuSerial. Indexing/abstracting usually covers material at the article/chapter level.

☐ monographic co-editions are intended for either non-subscribers or libraries which intend to purchase a second copy for their circulating collections.

☐ monographic co-editions are reported to all jobbers/wholesalers/approval plans. The source journal is listed as the "series" to assist the prevention of duplicate purchasing in the same manner utilized for books-in-series.

☐ to facilitate user/access services all indexing/abstracting services are encouraged to utilize the co-indexing entry note indicated at the bottom of the first page of each article/chapter/contribution.

☐ this is intended to assist a library user of any reference tool (whether print, electronic, online, or CD-ROM) to locate the monographic version if the library has purchased this version but not a subscription to the source journal.

☐ individual articles/chapters in any Haworth publication are also available through the Haworth Document Delivery Service (HDDS).

Dignity and Old Age

CONTENTS

ABOUT THE EDITORS

Robert Disch, MA, is Director of Intergenerational Programs, Brookdale Center on Aging, Hunter College, New York. He is the co-editor of *Intergenerational Approaches in Gerontology: Implications for Education, Policy, and Practice* (The Haworth Press, Inc., 1997).

Rose Dobrof, DSW, is Founding Director of the Brookdale Center on Aging and Emerita Professor, Brookdale Professor of Gerontology at Hunter College, New York. A nationally known authority in the field of aging, she is the editor of the *Journal of Gerontological Social Work* (The Haworth Press, Inc.) and Co-Chair of the U.S. Committee for the Celebration of the United Nations Year of the Older Person.

Harry R. Moody, PhD, is Executive Director of the Brookdale Center on Aging, Hunter College, New York, where he teaches gerontology and bioethics. A philosopher by background, he is the author of *The Five Stages of the Soul* (Doubleday, 1997).

Dedication to Ellsworth G. Stanton III

This volume is respectfully and lovingly dedicated to Ellsworth G. Stanton III. The conference, *Aging with Dignity*, on which we base this book, was Mr. Stanton's idea, and his twenty-two years as Executive Director of the James N. Jarvie Commonweal Service were informed by his steadfast and whole-hearted commitment to his mission of developing programs and services for older people which would, among other things, protect the dignity of all whom the Jarvie Service helped, even if mental impairment and chronic illness and physical incapacity became their fate. Indeed all of Mr. Stanton's adult life was devoted to service to others, a calling which articulated in quotidian activities Mr. Stanton's deeply held religious beliefs, his bedrock faith, and his certainty that all human beings, regardless of age or gender or circumstances, deserved to be treated with dignity, deserved the opportunity to grow and flourish as individuals and as members of our human society.

A biographic note about Mr. Stanton. He is a son of the Midwest, born in Evanston, Illinois, and a graduate of Roosevelt University in Chicago. He served in the United States Army during World War II. He is a ruling elder in the Presbyterian Church (USA), a trustee of the New York Theological Seminary, a member of the Board of the Presbyterian Senior Services and of the Federation of Protestant Welfare Agencies and was president of the John Milton Society for the Blind. In 1995 he was a delegate to the White House Conference on Aging, and at this writing is on the Executive Committee of the U.S. Committee for the United Nations Year of Older Persons, 1999.

[Haworth co-indexing entry note]: "Dedication to Ellsworth G. Stanton III." Dobrof, Rose. Co-published simultaneously in *Journal of Gerontological Social Work* (The Haworth Press, Inc.) Vol. 29, No. 2/3, 1998, pp. xv-xvi; and: *Dignity and Old Age* (ed: Robert Disch, Rose Dobrof, and Harry R. Moody) The Haworth Press, Inc., 1998, pp. xiii-xiv. Single or multiple copies of this article are available for a fee from The Haworth Document Delivery Service [1-800-342-9678, 9:00 a.m. - 5:00 p.m. (EST). E-mail address: getinfo@haworthpressinc.com].

xiii

The list of Mr. Stanton's activities, offices held, and honors bestowed is a long one, and the paragraph above highlights only a few. Now retired from his position as Executive Director of the Jarvie Commonweal Service, Mr. Stanton continues, in a variety of ways, his life of service to others, his efforts to improve the society–here and internationally–in which human beings grow up and grow old.

Mr. Stanton joins the authors of the papers in this volume and the members of the Editorial Board of the *Journal of Gerontological Social Work* in our hope that our readers will find the book helpful to them in their daily practice and even inspirational to them as they think about the people with whom they work. And Harry R. Moody and I dedicate the book to Ellsworth Stanton in recognition of the work he has done and the good life he leads, and in the certainty that he will continue to be a force for good in all that he does.

Rose Dobrof, DSW

Foreword

This volume is the outgrowth of a day-long conference on "Dignity and Aging" supported by the Jarvie Commonweal Fund and co-sponsored by the Brookdale Center on Aging of Hunter College. The Conference brought together gerontologists along with practitioners from a variety of fields in order to examine a central, if often overlooked idea: the meaning of dignity and its implications for how we look upon old age and older people.

This two-fold orientation of the Conference–the ideal of dignity as well as its practice–was repeatedly in the minds of those who presented papers. The two-fold orientation appeared in the questions posed by those who deliberated about dignity and age: for instance, does age in itself convey some kind of dignity or entitlement to respect? How can we define or understand the meaning of the word "dignity" today? How does the dignity of age relate to the position of people across the entire lifespan, including children and those in midlife? What can we learn about dignity from cross-cultural considerations, from religion, or from literature?

Questions about dignity are not merely abstract. The ideal of human dignity conveys important implications for how we treat older people at the level of practice–for example, in health care or social services–and also for our policies governing work and retirement as well as entitlements and benefits. Individuals and families, as well as philanthropy and government, have a role in assuring dignity in age, and professionals in the aging service network can enhance the quality of their care by appreciating the multiple meanings of dignity across different sectors of society.

[Haworth co-indexing entry note]: "Foreword." Dobrof, Rose, and Harry R. Moody. Co-published simultaneously in *Journal of Gerontological Social Work* (The Haworth Press, Inc.) Vol. 29, No. 2/3, 1998, pp. xvii-xviii; and: *Dignity and Old Age* (ed: Robert Disch, Rose Dobrof, and Harry R. Moody) The Haworth Press, Inc., 1998, pp. xv-xvi. Single or multiple copies of this article are available for a fee from The Haworth Document Delivery Service [1-800-342-9678, 9:00 a.m. - 5:00 p.m. (EST). E-mail address: getinfo@haworthpressinc.com].

xv

Participants and presenters at the Conference did not shrink from hard questions about dignity: can we really measure it or define it? Is it an elusive goal and can we afford it? How do we put into practice the behavior that we have come to believe is so essential for the respect and well-being of older people.

The questions will continue, but this volume represents an important step forward in framing the issues and in challenging us all to commit ourselves to assuring dignity for all those in the last stage of life.

Rose Dobrof, DSW
Harry R. Moody, PhD

Dignity Over the Life Course

Robert Coles, MD

I was trained in pediatrics, child psychiatry and child psychoanal-ysis, none of which qualifies me to address the topic of aging. My first memories as a clinician go back to the Children's Hospital in Boston during the last polio epidemic we'll ever see. At the time I was a resident there and I was taking care of children who were paralyzed . . . some of them were even in iron lungs. I distinctly remember, even then when I myself was young. Age, of course, varies depending on one's own age. At that time I seemed much older than these youngsters who were paralyzed, but in fact I was in my middle and late 20's and not that much older from my perspective now.

What I remember is some of their parents and especially the case of one girl who would die in an iron lung. I remember her grand-mother, who was the only one who could talk with her and give her some solace as she faced the terrible task of dealing with herself in a machine that was breathing for her as her life was ebbing away. She was from a privileged family and only 16 years old and out of the blue polio had arrived and soon would take her.

That connection between the grandmother, who was brought in by the young lady's parents in the sure knowledge that only she could comfort her, and that young woman–she was stuck in my mind, filed away as I dealt with all my other responsibilities then in the years that would follow and as I learned to do the kind of work I did. I would end up in the South in the early 1960's, running an Air Force psychiatric hospital and in turn would soon enough be a witness to school desegregation in New Orleans.

[Haworth co-indexing entry note]: "Dignity Over the Life Course." Coles, Robert. Co-published simultaneously in *Journal of Gerontological Social Work* (The Haworth Press, Inc.) Vol. 29, No. 2/3, 1998, pp. 1-12; and: *Dignity and Old Age* (ed: Robert Disch, Rose Dobrof, and Harry R. Moody) The Haworth Press, Inc., 1998, pp. 1-12. Single or multiple copies of this article are available for a fee from The Haworth Document Delivery Service [1-800-342-9678, 9:00 a.m. - 5:00 p.m. (EST). E-mail address: getinfo@ haworthpressinc.com].

1

Now, when I talk about that I always talk about one little girl, Ruby Bridges. Her very name is a symbolic invitation to what school desegregation meant–Ruby Bridges, who would desegregate an elementary school that was totally boycotted as a result of her entrance to that school by the white population. She would march by mobs every day in order to attend the school all by herself and would be greeted by threats and swear words and whatever. I've chronicled all this in my *Children of Crisis* series and in *The Moral Life of Children* and in *The Spiritual Life of Children*.

Why do I bring her up now? I mentioned from the very beginning Ruby's grandmother. In the first writing I did about her, those children were from Afro-American families, four of them in this case. They were initiating a difficult, dangerous pathway into the all-white schools of a cosmopolitan port city against terrific resistance that necessitated the President of the United States convening federal marshals to protect these families because the police in New Orleans and the State Police in Louisiana would not protect these children.

As I met these families, I encountered in family after family–not only those four families but other families that came to their assistance–I met elderly people who I began to realize were the moral and spiritual mainstays of these families. There is no other way to describe it.

Ruby Bridges would have been taken out of this predicament by her own parents–and they've said so–I'm saying nothing that they haven't said again and again. Were it not for Mrs. Bridge's mother, Ruby's Grandmother, who said "*No Way.*"

Now this is a family that came from the Delta of Mississippi. They were as poor as can be. The mother and father–never mind the grandparents–did not know how to read or write. And the same thing went for these other families who were plucked by a federal judge because of a residential qualification. That was the only qualification that he called upon in order to begin this process, six years after the 1954 decision of the Supreme Court.

Ruby's parents were as vulnerable as people could be: by race, by class, occupation, education, whatever. The father worked in a gas station. When the owner of the gas station found out who he was he fired him. They did not go on welfare: there was no welfare then for them. They scraped by. The community gathered around the Bridges family and the other three families and initiated desegregation in the McDonough 19 School. Ruby had the France School all to herself. Can you imagine a six year old girl going through mobs five days a week to go into a school that was totally boycotted? For a whole school year? This is out of the work of Franz Kafka, actually.

I was trying to find out why. I could be spend a long time trying to explain how I, working in an Air Force hospital in Mississippi, connected with these families and got involved with them and did my work, but I did. I was led to them by a woman by the name of Leontine Luke, who is now 87 years old, even then she was getting along as she put it to me. And I'll tell you, I thought her prospects were not so good.

She was remarkably overweight; she told me she had high blood pressure; and a clinical mind like mine even then could come to the conclusions. I saw her last year and she said to me, she was smarter than I ever thought she was, she said "You never thought I'd make it, did you?" I said, Make it to what? She said "Well, to 60, never mind 100!" So I said are you going to make it to 100? She said "Maybe." I said, "Oh, I have no doubt, now!"

But she shepherded those four families and she told me as I was getting to know them, she said "Do you want to find out about the strength of these families?" which I was beginning to remark upon. She said "You talk to those grandparents." And so I talked to those grandparents and found out about these families.

I found out that Ruby had been delivered by her great aunt, the sister of her grandmother, and that I was the first doctor that this family had ever met. They'd never met a pediatrician before, let alone an obstetrician. They had borne their children in the Delta of Mississippi and come into New Orleans because of the mechanization of agriculture. They were field hands, tenant farmers. But most of all I found out about their moral and psychological and spiritual strength, you bet I did. I was talking to children who had to go through mobs and did so well, so well. And a mind like mine is not trained to understand that. A mind like mine is trained to understand psychopathology and medical pathology and has a hard time figuring out survival, let alone resilience.

So we notice defense mechanisms, those of us who know what that phrase means, not necessarily lucky people, and we look for symptoms and difficulties, and record them. And if the symptoms are not forthcoming that itself is a symptom. I explained this rather condescendingly one day to the school teacher who told me that she didn't understand how this little girl could go through what she had to go through every day just to get into the school building, and be so remarkably cheerful and calm, and thoughtful, and hard working at school, and doing so well. Well, I told that teacher, this is so long as we can put up with this, till something begins to happen.

One day my interest was piqued because I arrived at the school and the teacher said to me, "You know, we had some trouble at the school this morning. Ruby stopped in front of that mob." There were about ten armed, deputized agents of the federal government who took her in, federal marshals. There were usually 30 or 40 people. When I first saw that mob there were about a thousand, but they had filtered down to the hard-core resisters. The teacher said, "She stopped, for the first time. And the marshals kind of tugged at her toward the school building but she was talking to that crowd and she wouldn't go on until she finished what she had to say." And, as a result, the people surged toward her, not necessarily because they heard what she was saying, but because she had stopped. And the marshals had to draw their guns, which was the first time they had done that in a month. And they finally got her in the building and brought her up to her classroom whereupon the teacher asked her what had happened. And she said "Nothing!" You know what that means, these days: she was into denial. One says that with great concern. "Nothing," she said. Well, the teacher said "Ruby, something happened. I was looking out of the window and I saw you talking to those people and you haven't been doing that lately."

She said, "I wasn't talking to those people." More denial. "What were you doing, Ruby?" "I was talking to God," Ruby said. Whereupon the teacher decided not to pursue this any further. She had to refer to a higher authority–not God in this case, but me! And when I came there, she said "There's something wrong there. She was talking to the crowd, but she didn't admit it. She says that she was talking to God. I'm worried about her now." So, I said, "Well, I'll find out."

We went to their home, my wife and I, as I had been doing twice a week. That evening I sat at the kitchen table with Ruby. My mother was an artist. I've been interested all my life in children's drawings going back to when I was in pediatrics. And I collected them by the hundreds which have turned into the thousands. I sat with Ruby and she was drawing a picture of the school building, actually.

I said, Ruby, something happened in front of that building this morning, I heard. She said "What?" I said, "Well, you tell me." She said "What do you mean?" I said, "Well the teacher told me that you stopped and you talked to that mob. They got upset. The marshals had to pull you toward the building." She said "No, I told the teacher I wasn't talking to those people." I said, "Well Ruby, who were you talking to?" She said "I was talking to God." I said, "Ruby, do you talk to God a lot? Because I talk to patients at the McLean Hospital outside of Boston, a psychiatric facility, who talk to God a lot."

And I thought, I didn't expect this to be happening to a six year old, healthy child—healthy, that is psychologically. And she said "Well, I do, I talk to God a lot." I said, "What do you mean?" She said, "I . . . like to talk to God." I said, "Have you been talking to God a long time?" She said, "Oh, yes!" I said, "Well, I don't understand why you had to talk to God at that particular moment going into that school building." And she said, "Because I forgot to talk to him earlier." I said, "Would you explain this, Ruby?" And she said, "Well, you see . . . you see . . . when I get up, I say a prayer and when I'm coming to the school I say a prayer. And when I go home I say a prayer, and when I go to bed I say a prayer."

So I said to myself, "That's a lot of praying." And I said, "Ruby, that's a lot of praying!" She said, "I like to pray." So I said, "I still don't understand why you had to say your prayer right then and there." She said, "Because I saw those people." I said, "What has that got to do with your praying?" She said, "It has a lot to do with my praying, 'cause I pray for them!"

And I looked at her and said, "You pray for them?" She said, "Oh, I pray for them all the time!" And I said, "Ruby, why would you want to pray for them?" She said, "Well, don't you think they need praying for?"

Nothing in my entire intellectual and medical life, not to mention

psychiatric and psychoanalytic life, had given me the least preparation for that kind of answer. But, undeterred and relentless as people
like me can often get–unfortunately with those we want to poke
around with–I said, "Ruby, I can understand that you might want to
pray for them or that they need praying for, but I'm not quite sure
that you of all people–despite your desire to pray for them–would
really wish to do so." She said, "Well, I'm the one who hears what
they say." I didn't know what to do with this, other than push on.
And I asked her what she said in her prayers. She said, "Oh, I say
what my grandmama tells me to say."

I said, what does she tell you to say? "She says . . . Ruby, you
pray for those people. And you pray for them like this. You say this
to those people. You say to God, please God, try to forgive them,
'cause they don't know what they're doing." I paused and said, "Is
that what you say?" She said, "That's what I say all the time." I
thought to myself, "I think this has been said before." This has a
faintly familiar ring to it. I said, "Ruby, is there any particular reason
you say that prayer?" She said, "Well, my grandma knows . . . my
grandmama . . . my grandmama, my grandma knows . . ." I said,
"How does she know?" She said, "She goes to church, and she
memorizes"–Grandmother couldn't read–"and she memorizes, and
she makes me memorize."

My wife and I used to go to that church, and let me tell you it
wasn't air-conditioned, and it would go on for sometimes two, two
and a half hours. This is what was called *Hard Praying*! *Hard
Praying*! Ruby's grandmother and grandfather and a lot of elderly
people in that community would husband these people into their
church and nurse them into that church. And while there they would
sing–oh, would they sing! And Ruby, through her grandparents, had
learned about Isaiah and Jeremiah, the Prophets of Israel and about
Jesus and his life and Ruby had been told by her grandmother
especially that if there was a mob in front of Jesus, that he'd prayed
for them. And she should try to do likewise. You talk about a moral
tradition being handed down in a family.

Ruby's grandmother had told her that she stood for something.
That her responsibility now was beyond that of a child or her own
education, that she stood in line for her people. A moral lesson
handed down to a six year old child by a woman who did what? A

woman then in her sixties, who had brought up many of her own children, who had worked in the houses of the well-to-do in the garden district, watching them, and listening to them and learning from them and carrying on a working life and a lived family life and inspiring others that they must work hard–that they must pray–that they must live worthy lives.

I write these things up. You'll find it mentioned in that early writing, especially about grandparents. But it took me some time to appreciate all this. I began to understand that never more searchingly than when I went out to New Mexico to work with the children of Spanish-speaking people in the northern communities north of Santa Fe, where I couldn't talk to these children without being scrutinized first by their grandparents and sometimes by their great-grandparents. The parents deferred to age and held up age. It was similar when I worked with Pueblo children and Navajo children, where age is the essence in these families of dignity, as that word is used today. How did Walker Percy put it at the end of his wonderful first novel, *The Moviegoer*, "We hand one another along . . ." It's a beautiful moment: to be handed along. This, these families knew as I would knock on doors and talk to school teachers. The school teachers gave me the first clue. North of Albuquerque and further north of Santa Fe: "You better talk to the elderly ones." They call them the old ones. They're the ones who are either going to say up or down.

And so I found sitting and talking to elderly people with a new kind of intent. Initially, to enlist their support, to get their approval for my purposes as observer of children. But eventually I would learn to listen to them for their own sake. To learn from them, even. I will tell you some of the most moving moments now in my teaching life up there in Cambridge. In the midst of teaching literature, teaching novels and poetry and short stories to students in a crowded undergraduate course. The most moving moment for me, but really because it's so moving for the students, is to read some of these "moments" as I transcribed them.

In 1972 or 1973 *The New Yorker* published one of those moments under the title of "Una Anciana." It's in *The Old Ones From Mexico*. Talk about an elderly book . . . it's been in print now for 25 years—which is a great kind of grandparent kind of book in publishing life.

Mr. Shawn was then the editor of *The New Yorker* and this piece came out around the time that the President of the United States was under some . . . duress. One of the great privileges of being elderly in some of those northern New Mexico communities is they've never heard of the President of the United States. And in that particular time in American history I sort of envied them.

But in any event I sent this "Una Anciana" piece to Shawn and he ran it as a profile of a humble, elderly lady and her moments as she thought she was dying, actually. And they were flooded with letters from people who were comparing her to Mr. Nixon. And Mr. Shawn said "Do you think you might want to tell that we've been flooded as we haven't in a long time with mail from people who for some reason find in her some dignity and some importance at this time when the country is in such political jeopardy . . . moral jeopardy?" I'll never forget this conversation with Mr. Shawn. I was living at the time in Albuquerque, and I said to Mr. Shawn, "I don't think I want to tell her about Mr. Nixon and the jeopardy that we're in." "Ahh," he said, "Well, just tell her that we all were interested to meet her." And whom did they meet? They met a woman of enormous spiritual strength. An even-tempered person with a wonderful sense of humor, weathered by years, frail in certain ways. But strong, so strong. And someone again, who was transmitting the values, the received values of her people on to another generation much in need of them.

Alex Harris is a photographer with whom I've worked for years and now working on a magazine called *Double Take*, which features photography as well as non-fiction and fiction in poetry. Alex took extraordinary pictures of some of these elderly people, and then he and I would work with Eskimos in Alaska. There is a picture he took of one of my sons and me talking with an elderly Eskimo, the elder of that community, Norvic. The picture shows my son and me—my son at the time was 9 years old. We were transfixed by this man as he was telling us about the life of this village, transmitting to us factuality, observations, experiences, impressions, hopes, worries. And yes, an entire education about the landscape, about a people, and some very shrewd observations about another kind of people, namely as he called it "those from the lower 48" who come up here and why they come up here. No training in psychology, not even an ability to read or write.

Ruby's grandmother didn't know how to read or write but boy, she knew how to pray, and forgive–forgiveness and understanding. In fact, my wife once pointed out to me, she said "You know, here are people who are so hard pressed and so vulnerable and who have lived long and tough lives, and they can forgive." And she said, "What would you do if you had to go into the Harvard Faculty Club and there was a mob blocking your way? We can be sure I wouldn't be praying for them, can't we be sure?" Maybe trying to analyze them. Maybe calling the police and getting a lawyer, which the Bridges family couldn't do. Mobilizing psychiatric language and probably writing ten articles about what I went through. No prayer, though.

I am not trying to say that there aren't appropriate moments for lawyers and the police and the language of the social sciences and even some articles. But I will say as I don't think that in so many of our elderly people they have learned what they have learned, learned the huge lessons of life. Our universities don't know how to acknowledge that sufficiently, I regret to say. They acknowledge the brilliance of youth, but not necessarily, unfortunately, the wisdom of age. How sad.

One of the things I love to teach, if I can call it a thing, is Tillie Olson's story "Tell Me a Riddle" about an elderly couple and what they have gone through. I love to teach "The Death of Ivan Illych" by Tolstoy. And I love to teach "Master and Man" by Tolstoy. These writers tried to come to terms in their wise way with the elderly even as one can come to terms as you do with the elderly by listening to them, maybe even listening to oneself and remembering all that one has learned. Learned not in courses, but through acquiring the great lessons of life through experience, through disappointments, and pain and suffering which all of us in our various ways are privy to.

Some of the saddest moments I have, among a privileged group of students in this great university in Cambridge, Massachusetts, some of the saddest moments are when I sit with students and realize how little contact they've had with their own parents. That's

one problem with grandparents: how little they know and therefore
have been given.

I am now finishing up some work I've done with elderly people.
What have I been doing? Well, the title of it is "Old and On Their
Own." I go and talk to elderly people who, regardless of their
physical condition and their social and economic condition are at
home, being kept there by a variety of services. And I've been
working again with photographers, including Alex Harris. This is a
long debt I owe to the Commonwealth Fund, because I did these
interviews over the years and I'm finally getting around to sending
this off to a publisher.

But, I'm glad that I've waited, because it's kept me in contact
with some of these people: someone who just turned 100, people
who are counting the years until they're 100 and are over that 90
year mark–young people in their early 80's–people looking back
who have educated me about this century, its politics, its social life.
Through their memories, I am witness to what America has been
like and continues to be like as they observe it and remark upon it.
And I also must tell you about what some of my Harvard College
students have learned to do which is a wonderful thing. They do
community service and work with young people as tutors and men-
tors. They have learned to take children from the Boston schools
and the Cambridge schools, individually and in groups, to nursing
homes and to the elderly, so that those children can leap across the
generations and inspire–what? Storytelling? Respect? To look up to
someone and be taught by someone is to give someone something.
Even as one gets back of course, by being told and told. To watch
children leave an elementary school and go to a nursing home not
far away and be part of these two worlds joining and to hear elderly
people telling these children about the Second World War and the
First World War and this president and that president.

I remember one elderly lady telling a group of three children that
she remembered taking her children out of school to go see Franklin
D. Roosevelt as he was being driven through the streets of Boston
with Governor James M. Curley at his side. By the time she got
finished with that story these children were looking. And she said
"You go back and find out about that President. Find out what he
did . . . and why I was so excited about him," she said. Wonderful

teaching, because those children went back and asked their teacher, "Who was this Franklin D. Roosevelt? And why was that elderly lady so excited about him?" There's a way to learn history that won't be forgotten! Of course, these children liven up the nursing home and in certain individual homes are a breath of fresh air, aren't they? Ears to be filled, eyes to watch, and that connection.

What else is there in this life? What matters more than connection? That connection works. And would that we knew more about this and enhanced it more, and would that our universities and medical schools paid more attention, not to the elderly as a problem, as a mass of pathology only, but as a people of enormous moral and spiritual and psychological resources that are there courtesy of life. As St. Augustine said, "Let us live our lives not with our lips, but with our behavior." When you've been living to 70, or 80, or 90, there is a lot of behavior there–there are lessons to be learned and they in turn can be transmitted.

So, I am here to tell you really what you already know and to echo it from the other side, from a lifetime spent with the young even now as a teacher. I teach now not only college students but I'm also a volunteer teacher in a Boston ghetto school and I go to that fifth grade class and find that when I get those children talking about their grandparents, a certain solemnity and pause takes place in that classroom. These are the people who still wield under some instances of moral anarchy, still wield some authority. Who still can intervene and walk on a street and induce a moment of pause in people who otherwise don't stop at anything to get what they want.

There are implications in all this, I can tell you. Even abstract implications for public policy. I often wonder, as I work in certain communities, what we might do in a systematic way with some of the older people in that community on behalf of certain causes and needs. These are people who are usually overlooked. But, whether we overlook them or not, these are people who still have neverthe-less significance in particular families and in their neighborhoods, people who therefore we are to attend for that reason alone. For the obvious reason that they are our fellow citizens and this is a destina-tion to which, let us hope and pray, we are all heading. How we measure any society surely is a function–I'm reaching into the obvious here–of how we treat those who are vulnerable, whether they be very young or very old, the sick, the needy, in one way or another.

There is a lot of emphasis I know these days on the psychopathology that takes place in the elderly. Well, you could study the psychopathology that takes place in many populations, including, I might add, psychopathologists. But I find it more interesting and important for us to emphasize the reality of what depression can sometimes mean. Why shouldn't some of us be depressed in view of some of the things that are taking place around us? I have noticed when some of those children go into those nursing homes in Boston or when I take them to visit certain elderly people I know, what is called depression quickly gives way to smiles and cheer, and a lovely moment or two. And I don't think this is all that mysterious, nor is it fake nor will it necessarily go away. It can be sustained and maintained. There are people who come to those homes that I've been visiting who have enormous vitality—visiting nurses and dieticians, and bearers of food, social workers, and again some of those kids. My students and their children.

This is a parade of connection in which young people and some old people in turn connect with people yet older still. And there's something very fine about this and moving. And it's been a privilege to observe it and to try to understand it: for example, my centenarian friend as he gets ready to appear on the *Today* show. Not quite 100, he says "I'm just waiting for that moment!" He and others. As he jokes with me, he said "You looking forward to that?" I said, "Oh Lord, *Never*! It'll never happen." "How did it happen?" I ask him. And in reply I get a wisdom that transcends medicine because they usually tell me about all the reasons that they shouldn't have made it. By the time I talk to enough people like that I'm very skeptical about my own profession and it's possibilities because I think to myself, I was trained to write off all these people and here they are. It causes me to scratch my head and wonder why. But that, of course, is one of the great lessons that people can teach other people. To ask why. To look at the world with a certain awe and wonder. To undo that self-confident smugness that some of us are heir to either occupationally or for some other set of reasons.

Why Dignity in Old Age Matters

Harry R. Moody, PhD

IS DIGNITY OBSOLETE?

The story of Oedipus begins with the riddle of the Sphinx: "What is the creature that walks on four legs in the morning, two legs at noon, and three legs in the evening?" The answer of course is a human being, a creature who crawls on four legs as an infant, walks on two legs as an adult, then walks with a cane in old age. After solving this riddle Oedipus goes on to achieve kingship, supreme symbol of power and dignity in the world. But, as both Sophocles and Freud remind us, in his ascent to worldly power Oedipus carries with him a terrible secret about his own fate. When destiny finally catches up with him, he eventually loses his position in the world. In old age, Oedipus becomes a wanderer, a man with no place in society. He loses his dignity altogether.

The story of Oedipus, like the riddle of the sphinx, is a parable about the life cycle, from infancy to old age. Sophocles wrote the last play, *Oedipus at Colonnus*, depicting the aged king when the playwright himself was over 90 years old. Oedipus, then, is reminder of a universal threat: namely, that after struggling from infantile dependency to achieve adult dignity–the upright posture–we may once again, in the twilight of life, find ourselves degraded. Whether by stroke, by Alzheimer's, by poverty or by whatever cause, we stand at risk of losing everything achieved over a lifetime. Each of us, however, dimly, carries this unspoken awareness during our

[Haworth co-indexing entry note]: "Why Dignity in Old Age Matters." Moody, Harry R. Co-published simultaneously in *Journal of Gerontological Social Work* (The Haworth Press, Inc.) Vol. 29, No. 2/3, 1998, pp. 13-38; and: *Dignity and Old Age* (ed: Robert Disch, Rose Dobrof, and Harry R. Moody) The Haworth Press, Inc., 1998, pp. 13-38. Single or multiple copies of this article are available for a fee from The Haworth Document Delivery Service [1-800-342-9678, 9:00 a.m. - 5:00 p.m. (EST). E-mail address: getinfo@haworthpressinc.com].

13

lives. Life can end badly: fear of aging is still rooted in this grim understanding.

Dignity in old age matters because every one of us carries this sense of vulnerability and because we fear becoming less than ourselves in the last stage of life. Contemporary debates about assisted suicide, concern over treatment of the frail elderly, and anxieties about the future of Social Security all revolve around a primal fear: loss of dignity in old age.

But the concept of dignity in old age is not a simple idea. "Dignity" as an idea has a long and important history in ethics but it does not denote a single essence. On the contrary, the meaning of dignity is complex, ambiguous and multivalent–something akin to what Wittgenstein suggests in his example the word "game": that is, a cluster or network of meanings captured by the metaphor of "family resemblance." The essentialist quest for conceptual purity beyond history and change is futile, Wittgenstein warns us. Better to look at the use of ideas in order to probe the depth of their meaning.

Dignity in old age is inescapably an ethical ideal, a moral touchstone: above all, it is a term of approbation and appraisal still used widely even in a culture like our own where we find it difficult to agree on its meaning. Dignity is a standard by which we measure conduct, our own or others. We call on the idea of dignity when we describe an act as "undignified" and thereby condemn it as unworthy of us or unworthy of the agent who acts in an undignified fashion.

But is "dignity" then merely a fact about rhetoric and moral discourse? Is it simply a fact that we sometimes find ourselves condemning acts as "undignified" and that the point of this condemnation seems to express, however vaguely, something more than merely aesthetic judgment? This would be an emotivist, or relativist way of interpreting the meaning of dignity. But then, what does an appeal to "dignity" serve to express? How can we make sense of it and how do we justify employing dignity as a moral category? Is dignity after all distinct from related ethical ideas such as "rights," "respect for others," "autonomy," and so on? More provocatively, do we really need an appeal to dignity, or has the word become a mere placeholder, a rhetorical relic superseded by more relevant moral categories? Finally, when we speak of dignity in old age, are we denoting an "ideal old age" or simply calling upon a rudimentary ethical appeal to uphold basic human decency?

Appeals to basic decency are never to be despised. There is a familiar "minimalist" approach to dignity and age that creeps into the language of public piety. This minimalist approach is evident in rhetorical appeals that invoke images of elderly people who are victimized or exploited–as in tales of elder abuse or old people eating dogfood due to poverty. This appeal is grounded in venerable rhetorical tradition. After all, in the Fifth Commandment, the Bible reminds us to "honor" our fathers and mothers and to "rise up" before the hoary head of the old man, to pay respect to the elders of the tribe.

Minimalist appeals to dignity serve as an ethical "floor" or restraint on dehumanizing treatment of the very old. After all, it is said that we can "do no less" than to treat the old with respect, even if we are not quite clear about how one renders respect based on chronological age. Does it mean giving up a seat on the bus? Addressing older people as "Mr. Jones" or "Mrs. Smith?" Behaving in (modestly) deferential ways toward gray-heads in our midst? We cannot be sure. Cultural consensus unravels quickly, but we assent to dignity as a "good thing" even though we may secretly suspect that the concept of dignity lacks specific moral content. Like vacuous campaigns on behalf of "self-esteem" or "civil society,"the moral dimensions of dignity are a mile wide and an inch deep.

The Obsolescence of the Concept of Dignity. The sentimental coloration of appeals to dignity calls forth a deeper fear: perhaps the whole idea of dignity in age is simply obsolete. Today, at the close of the 20th century, the concept of dignity does suffer from a certain archaic connotation. As with problematic terms of appraisal like "gentleman" or "virginity," we are tempted to think of "dignity" as irrelevant, as an outdated ethical ideal, in contrast, say, to psychologically more appealing moral imperatives like as "sensitivity" or "inclusiveness." It's all right to treat older people with "dignity" if treating them that way makes them feel better (since feelings are what count). And, yes, it's desirable to include the old (no one wants to be accused of ageism). So, yes indeed, there are obligations toward the elders, but obligations don't entail appeals to dignity. We might in fact ask: If we're doing everything else right, ethically speaking, then why worry about dignity at all?

The problem may be even worse than this bald question implies. By appealing to dignity, by appealing to something beyond sensitivity and inclusiveness, we presume too much. Doesn't an appeal to the idea of dignity imply a kind of cultural imperialism, the hegemony of smug, tongue-clucking disapproval? If dignity is to count seriously, then older people *themselves* might fail to act in dignified fashion, and so we would find ourselves disapproving of them, becoming "judgmental" (the worst of sins in liberal society).

We then come close, one imagines, to the same oppressive attitude that, say, would dismiss rap music as "undignified" while favoring "dignified" dress for social occasions (a classical concert?) "Elitism" and "judgmentalism" are not attractive options at a time when egalitarianism and the ideal of tolerance reign supreme. But if the concept of dignity is to mean anything at all, if it is something more than rhetorical inflation, then don't we run the danger of importing unjustified class distinctions or unsupported claims of moral superiority? When we speak about the dignity of old age, aren't we invoking claims about an attitude to life that has become indefensible or culturally obsolete?

These are disturbing questions that Marx, or Nietzsche, or Foucault might have asked about any attempt to revive dignity as a category of moral discourse. If we take those questions seriously, then we are perilously close to deflating the rhetoric of dignity altogether. In its place, an easy-going tolerance (sometimes dressed up as "post-modernism") comes to our rescue: we can have our cake and eat it too. Perhaps older people, on this argument, are entitled to act in ways that seem appropriate *to them*–in ways that seem "dignified"–just like wearing a tie to dine out in a restaurant. We will respect that behavior and treat the old with dignity. Their preferences exert no claims on the rest of us, but we honor them all the same.

This example of a dress code underscores the core strategy of using "tolerance" as a tactic to vindicate contradictory claims about dignity. "Live and let live" goes the response of the relativist. We can even honor dignity so enthusiastically that we endorse a multiplicity of ideas about what dignity will mean: let a hundred flowers bloom.

But in our enthusiasm for tolerance, let us admit one small point. We are tempted to tolerate contrasting claims about dignity because we're confused by the whole subject and because we find it difficult to take *competing* claims about dignity with moral seriousness at all. The whole matter ends up as a problem for "Miss Manners," not a question for the ethics consultant. And there lies the price of conventionalism and "postmodern" tolerance, which increasingly defines the social and philosophical landscape of the world in which we live (Harvey, 1989).

We cannot easily vindicate the substantive ideal of late life dignity. Appeals to dignity fall apart in an era when moral claims of all kinds become relativized and turned into matters of mere convention. Dignity becomes, in the end, an aesthetic matter, as with all categories of post-modern sensibility. We have "saved" the ideal of dignity at the price of emptying it of substantive ethical content and making it a purely individual decision or a matter of taste. Your dignity or mine–may they both be alive and well.

I have posed these questions and offered preliminary arguments against dignity not because I agree with them–I do not–but because the goal of this chapter, and of this entire book, is to say why dignity in old age continues to matter, to make it clear why something crucial is at stake in the idea of dignity in old age. Part of my purpose here is intellectual archeology: an effort to uncover conceptual artifacts whose meanings were once obvious to our ancestors but which are increasingly obscure or even archaic, as the ideal of "dignity" seems to many of us today.

My strategy is close to the method pursued by Christopher Lasch, in his critique of the "culture of narcissism"; or the analysis of Philip Rieff in analyzing "the triumph of the therapeutic"; or to Peter Berger in describing "the obsolescence of the concept of honor." In another vein, the task is one of moral archeology as found, in different ways, in the work of Michel Foucault and Alasdair MacIntyre. Just as MacIntyre argued that, historically speaking, we live in a cultural epoch where the idea of virtue no longer makes sense, so I want to begin by acknowledging the ways in which the idea of dignity in old age has ceased to make sense. But in the end,

I want to rehabilitate some elements from the core of dignity in old age and to lay a groundwork for understanding why dignity is important for policy and practice. Specific details of the concept are expounded by other writers in this book.

Here I emphasize this moral dimension of dignity because it helps put ethical claims up front for serious debate. Dignity in old age matters, I will argue, because dignity amounts to something more than a matter of aesthetics or taste. The idea of dignity necessarily involves a *moral* term of appraisal, a term that is somehow linked to our sense of the meaning of the last stage of life.

On the face of it, this claim might seem implausible. We look in vain for any discussion of dignity in the academic literature of gerontology. On the contrary, non-moral terms of appraisal are used extensively, though without much philosophical explication of their meaning. Gerontology is replete with appeals to ideas like "quality of life" or "life satisfaction"; the literature on aging policy is filled with discussions about "age-based entitlements" or "locus of control," which are often tied to a moral appraisal linked to age. Clearly, these concepts all bear a relation to the ideal of dignity, but the term "dignity" itself almost never appears except as a rhetorical appeal: as an ornament not to be considered seriously. But appeals to dignity are serious. Even rhetorical appeals (e.g., "death with dignity") remind us that important matters are at stake. Dignity is like the ghost at the Macbeth's banquet: invisible but potent in ways we may not imagine.

The idea that moral appraisal of dignity is linked to a substantive vision of the last stage of life seems especially problematic. We wonder: Does old age have an ideal form, a "proper" style of dignity (Christenson, 1978)? This question of whether there is, or ought to be, a moral ideal linked to old age as a distinct stage of life remains controversial. Leading gerontologists have argued the opposite. There have been articulate advocates of an "age-irrelevant society," like Bernice Neugarten or an "age-integrated society," like Matilda Riley (Riley and Riley, 1994). They are vigorous in their criticism of ill-treatment of the aged. But appeals to dignity play no part in their argument. On the contrary, achievement of an age-irrelevant society would signify the disappearance of distinctive rights and qualities linked to old age. The "dignity" of age would disappear as a term of moral appraisal. Dignity, if it means anything at all, corresponds to the removal of barriers and prejudices of all kinds. Since age-based expectations ("Act your age!") are such a barrier to progress, they should simply be removed, just as we ended mandatory retirement. The outcome of this campaign would make any age-based rights or duties appear as a pure anachronism. Under the new dispensation giving one's seat on the bus to an elderly person would no longer be a sign of respect (dignity?), but would be a put down, a kind of unacceptable stereotyping.

Age-associated dignity, then, is not only quaint but perhaps even dangerous. The idea of dignity, then, may be more obsolete than we had even imagined. On this (postmodern) account, dignity is to be replaced by a more sweeping agenda of human freedom. The "three boxes of life" (education, work, retirement) should be broken up in favor of a fluid, open-ended universality which marks the achievement of true human equality and opportunity. The rhetorical "dignity of age" might survive, but only as an unending capacity to remake ourselves at every stage of life, including the last. In this narrative, the postmodern life course is not only continuous or compatible with the dynamic tendency of modernity itself. Indeed, the postmodern life course represents the fulfillment of the Enlightenment project of liberation through autonomy–a point we will come back to. Dignity, in the older, pre-Enlightenment sense, would now be relegated to the dustbin of history, along with racism, sexism, ageism, and every other kind of prejudice.

If this account were the whole story, there would be no need for writing this book, or rather, the book itself would simply be unintelligible. Trying to take dignity seriously would make as much sense as an appeal for the revival of Greek mythology or medieval knighthood. But before we so quickly dispense with the concept of dignity, we would be well advised to better understand its logic and its many meanings. The historical account, including the postmodern narrative that debunks dignity, is not sufficient for that historical and linguistic purpose. We need instead to look in more detail at the taxonomy of dignity itself in its multiple meanings of moral appraisal.

MULTIPLE MEANINGS OF "DIGNITY"

It is a curious feature of the word "dignity" that as we apply the word to elderly people we can use it to judge *both* their own behavior and *also* actions taken with respect to them. In effect, there are two distinct frameworks involved here. To put it differently, dignity as a moral category encompasses both *self-regarding* and *other-regarding* behavior. We can say of an individual that he or she acts in an undignified manner (the self-regarding framework). Or we can say that another party–a service-provider, for instance–treats an elderly person in an undignified way: that is, disrespectfully (the other-regarding framework). It is part of my argument that these two dimensions are ineluctably linked to one another.

Both the self-regarding and the other-regarding sides of dignity revolve around a shared core meaning: namely, some idea of "showing respect." Failing the moral test of dignity means failing to show the right kind of respect: whether failing in self-respect or failing to treat others with the respect they deserve. But why do people, and especially why do old people, deserve some special kind of respect? And how is it ever possible to act in ways that violate self-respect? What is it about old age that demands conduct in keeping with this imperative of "showing respect?"

These questions require an answer that links self-regarding and other-regarding dimensions of dignity and respect for age. The linkage appears concretely in policies and practices that reflect how way we treat older people in our society, and it is to this context of policy and practice that we turn now.

Contemporary debates in aging often invoke the idea of dignity, whether explicitly or implicitly. We can begin with the "800 pound gorilla" of contemporary public policy, the matter of age-based entitlements. Today, for example, there is a vigorous debate about the future of Social Security and Medicare–primary examples of age-based entitlements. With the aging of the Baby Boom generation, and with continuing pressure to balance the federal budget, this debate over entitlements will surely continue. It is important to understand how appeals to dignity are part of the public debate around entitlements.

We note that in the context of American social policy, the largest entitlement programs are those based mainly on chronological age (Social Security and Medicare). Prevention of old age poverty has seemed an indispensable ingredient for late life dignity, and there is little doubt that social insurance programs have contributed to promoting that goal. But vigorous debate has surrounded preservation or expansion of age-based entitlements. Some have argued that these entitlements should be given not on the basis of chronological age but on the basis of need, perhaps through a means test. On the other side, many aging advocates believe that age-based entitlements are more likely to insure dignity than would needs-based entitlements, above all means-tested programs of any kind (Holstein, 1995). On this view, Medicare and Social Security, as programs of public provision, treat citizens with more dignity than, say, Medicaid or Food Stamps.

The argument here evokes earlier debates in the history of social welfare. Consider the polarity of justice versus charity as a moral basis for helping the poor. Advocates for the poor have long believed that services rendered by government as a matter of right and justice are more in keeping with the dignity of the poor than services rendered as private acts of charity by philanthropic groups.

This debate about age-based entitlements finds its parallel in debates over age-segregated service systems. In gerontology there has long been debate about whether elderly people preserve their dignity best in an "aging sub-culture"–whether a senior citizens center or a retirement community. To the extent that older people live in age-segregated settings by choice, they may find a certain dignity lacking in age-integrated settings. Those who choose to live in an age-segregated setting sometimes say it's simply less threatening to be with others of their own age. This is often a way of saying that self-esteem and self-respect is more easily sustained in a common culture shared by age-peers: a disguised invocation of dignity.

But not everyone has been persuaded by such appeals to dignity as a basis for age-segregation. Critics of age-segregated services wonder if the dignity of the aged is actually best preserved by ghetto-ization of elders. Others suggest that intergenerational, age-integrated programs might inculcate standards of respect on the part of younger people toward the old. If we believe that age-segregated settings are a kind of "grey ghetto," then we will work to break down those barriers and rely on age-segregated services only on a temporary provisional basis. Moreover, critics of nursing homes have argued that we need to develop institutional arrangements that are more responsive to human dignity than massive long-term care facilities can easily be. The popularity of home care and assisted living is part of this appeal for greater dignity along the continuum of care for dependent elderly (Miller & Wilson, 1991).

These debates around the meaning of dignity in entitlements or services are part of a wider concern over the status of the aged in modern societies. There are some who believe that age-based entitlements today express a stereotypical view of the elderly (as needy, dependent, vulnerable): an outdated "failure model" of aging which ought to give way to treatment in keeping with the empirical diversity and heterogeneity of the aged as a group. Similarly, there are those who argue that the treatment of elders under a rule-governed framework of public welfare inevitably fails to take account of–that is, to show respect for–individual needs and differences. Here too, the argument strikes a familiar chord. Under a regime of bureaucracy, it is said, people are treated as objects: that is, disrespectfully and in violation of their dignity. Proponents of this view naturally favor more reliance on either the marketplace or private charity and philanthropy with their greater possibilities for discretion and flexibility.

Finally, it is necessary to note the popular appeal of the idea of "death with dignity" in current debates over assisted suicide, an issue that affects the elderly more than any other group in our society. Critics have again and again pointed to nursing home care and to the treatment of elderly people in hospitals. The press is filled with horror stories about frail old people kept alive in conditions that seem dehumanizing. Dr. Kevorkian and the advocates of physician-assisted suicide insist that people should have the right to end a life deprived of dignity. A powerful segment of public opinion, both young and old, has been in agreement, which is why juries have failed to convict Dr. Kevorkian and why opinion surveys show a growing proportion of the public in favor of self-determined death. Appeals to dignity are an indispensable part of this crusade.

These debates in policy and practice are likely to persist. But opponents in debates over age-based entitlements, age-segregated housing, or assisted suicide often talk past each other and invoke appeals to dignity in ways that are confusing. In order to make sense of these debates it is helpful to sort out some of the multiple meanings of the idea of dignity.

I said earlier that dignity is not a simple idea or clearly defined concept but is rather a cluster or network of meanings captured by the metaphor of family resemblance. Birnbacher notes that "Even in its everyday use, then, and most noticeably in its legal use, there is no unitary and homogeneous concept of [human dignity], but rather a family of meanings, the members of which behave differently not only semantically but also syntactically" (Birnbacher, 1983, p. 115). What follows in the next section of this chapter is one taxonomy suggesting something of the range of meaning covered by the idea of dignity:

Self-Respect	vs.	Shame
Honor	vs.	Humiliation
Decorum	vs.	Inappropriate Behavior
Privacy	vs.	Exposure
Power	vs.	Vulnerability
Equality	vs.	Favoritism
Adulthood	vs.	Infantilization
Ego Integrity	vs.	Despair
Individuation	vs.	Objectification
Autonomy	vs.	Dependency

With debates over policy and practice in the background, let us examine more closely the polarities embedded in the concept of dignity, beginning with the first polarity. In this polarity *Self-respect* is contrasted with *Shame* (not the same thing as guilt). The polarity reminds us of the important point that most self-regarding actions have their roots in transactions of socialization that developmentally give rise to what we call the self. Simply put, we become who we are by seeing ourselves through the eyes of others. Shame, then, is a distinctive ingredient in the psychological construction of the self.

As children, when we did the wrong thing (say, wet our pants) we were held up to shame and ridicule and we then go on to internalize those feelings and carry them forward even as we age. It is for this reason that incontinence among the elderly is an assault on dignity: it evokes primal memories of shame.

In the philosophical literature on ethics the ideal of self-respect seems to involve much more than embarrassment or shame in the eyes of others. As a category of ethical appraisal self-respect is not simply a psychological phenomenon but rather the capacity to be part of a rational community and thus to see our own conduct through the eyes of another: to universalize our actions and so to feel ashamed of wrongdoing. In essence, it is Kant's idea of the categorical imperative and the Golden Rule, which he takes to be the foundation of morality.

The childhood experience of shame can be distinguished, though on a continuum of course, from the idea of honor, which arises at later ages in life. The word "honor" itself sounds quaint today, as Peter Berger noted, as if it might pertain to dueling or virginity. But honor need not be thought of as quaint at all. More broadly speaking, the polarity of *Honor* versus *Humiliation* simply evokes a connection between dignity and role performance requirements. Viewed in this way, the concept of honor is not as obsolete as it might sound. True, we don't support the institution of dueling today, but every society maintains role performance requirements. To fulfill a specific social role–student, parent, employee–is a basis for receiving honor (respect) from others. Conversely, to fail in those standards is a basis for humiliation and loss of dignity.

This point poses a distinctive question for gerontology. Are there any role performance requirements for old age or is old age rather a "roleless role," as Rosow maintained? Just as shame is ultimately a self-regarding emotion, so the concept of honor or humiliation is other-regarding. Honor and self-respect, then, are two poles (other-regarding and self-regarding) of ego identity at every point in the life course. We can be treated with honor or respect by others; but we can also feel shame or humiliation in the eyes of others. Once internalized, as Sartre observed, the "look" of the Other then takes on a life of its own: we feel shame or loss of self-respect regardless of whether our acts are visible to others.

The third polarity invites a still broader consideration of social perspective when we contrast *Decorum* with *Inappropriate behavior*. The importance of this distinction arises from the fact that not all social roles are well-defined. A "husband" is reasonably well-defined, for instance, but to be a guest at a party or to be a member of an audience are ill-defined roles. Still, certain actions depart from proper decorum and are blameworthy, causing loss of dignity. This observation raises a question about what it means to "act your age." Are there acts that are in keeping, or out of keeping, with some idea of decorum, some notion of what is "fitting" for an elderly person? For instance, can a 70-year old wearing a miniskirt be treated with dignity or can she act with dignity? In a time when young and old increasingly dress and act alike, it is not so obvious how these questions could be answered.

The polarity of *Privacy* and *Exposure* has special importance to the treatment of older patients in health care settings. Hospitals and nursing homes, for instance, often violate the dignity of patients by exposing their naked bodies to strangers or to the eyes of other patients without attention to any embarrassment this exposure might cause. Rosalie Kane has argued, the economy of nursing home life in America often doesn't permit single rooms. But should that practice be acceptable, or is it an assault on dignity? The result of the general refusal of single rooms is that privacy is routinely compromised on a continuing basis, and this violation of privacy is very often experienced as a loss of dignity. In a time when there is understandable ethical debate about the privacy of confidential medical records, it is useful to remember that the most fundamental ideas of privacy, exposure and dignity have been rooted in the visibility of the human body.

This allusion to issues of privacy in long-term care reminds us of the wider bureaucratic context of aging services. To speak of people in nursing homes or other "total institutions" (Goffman) underscores a familiar point about dignity in old age. When people are powerless, they lose their dignity in profound and far-reaching ways. In some very obvious way, the idea of dignity might be operationalized as "the right to complain." Whether in an egalitarian or a hierarchical society, I can only claim dignity as a person insofar as I retain a right to complain of ill-treatment. The slave has lost all dignity because he is treated as chattel and has no right to complain about anything. Slavery, then, is an extreme point on the polarity of *Power* versus *Vulnerability*. But examples from the world of long-term care make it clear how old people often lose their dignity when they can become frail and vulnerable or perhaps lose the right to make complaints for fear of retaliation.

In contemporary societies where the rule of law is paramount the need to protect the dignity of the old from abusive power often takes the form of equality before the law–hence, the polarity of *Equality* versus *Favoritism*, or idiosyncratic treatment. Again, we can see the importance of this distinction in the case of long-term care where some residents may be treated with more respect if they are able to tip staff members or buy services or otherwise obtain special privileges. In this sense, favoritism means treatment of people in ways that deviate from fair and equal treatment called for by virtue of their status as defined by the public rules of the institution. Equality, in this sense, does not forbid giving extra help to residents with mobility problems, but it does forbid giving extra services to residents who are "well-connected." We rightly fear a world where we can "buy" our dignity because we fear circumstances of vulnerability (including loss of money) that would radically reduce our bargaining power–as happened to Oedipus and King Lear in old age once they lost their kingship and became wandering beggars.

The story of Oedipus reminds us that the meaning of dignity in old age cannot be understood apart from the human life cycle encompassing all the ages of life. Even in modern societies, children do not have the same dignity (right to complain) as adults. To have full dignity–that is, to have full rights–is in a modern society to be a citizen; dignity in that sense belongs in its fullness to an adult, not to a child. In temporal or age-based terms, then, dignity denotes a status we move into as we grow up.

But what happens when we grow old? In legal terms, nothing at all. The 90-year is no more, and no less, a citizen than a 30-year old. But should old age bring frailty or, in cases of dementia, should age bring with it diminished mental capacity, then a predictable response by others is *Infantilization*: that is, the aged person is no longer treated with the respect of *Adulthood*. The polarity here does not point to a conspiracy of ageism but instead is rooted in the developmental status of dignity over the life cycle itself. Whenever we lose capacity–to control excretion or to maintain our memory– we lose a sense of adulthood, of basic dignity.

To speak about virtues rooted in the total life cycle is inevitably to recall the powerful vision of Erik Erikson. Erikson's famous "Eight Ages of Man" recognized in old age a basic polarity be- tween *Ego-integrity* and *Despair*. His thoughts on ego-integrity in late life are still among the most profound and moving ever ex- pressed on this subject:

> [Ego integrity] . . . is the acceptance of one's one and only life cycle as something that had to be and that, by necessity, per- mitted of no substitutions: it thus means a new, a different love of one's parents . . . Although aware of the relativity of all the various life styles which have given meaning to human striv- ing, the possessor of integrity is ready to defend the dignity of his own life style against all physical and economic threats. For he knows that an individual life is the accidental coinci- dence of but one life cycle with but one segment of history; and that for him all human integrity stands or falls with the one style of integrity of which he partakes.

Erikson's psychosocial theory of human development under- scores the way that psychological traits unfold in accordance with social and institutional practices: self-regarding and other-regarding behavior is thereby indissolubly linked. In the last stage of life, as at every other stage, each of us is set a task for which success is by no means guaranteed. In short, our dignity is at risk. In contrast to an easygoing, "postmodern" ethos of individualism, Erikson delin- eates the way in which social structure and history shapes our destiny and entails existential risks. But those risks, he reminds us, are not that of the solitary individual. Just as each age has its tasks and possibilities, so age-groups are intertwined. Dignity at the end of life constitutes a positive affirmation of the way generations are linked together.

But does old age then have a distinctive meaning of its own, some possibility that confers the possibility of integrity in the last stage of life? Carl Jung in his essay "The Stages of Life" wrote that

A human being would certainly not grow to be seventy or eighty years old if this longevity had no meaning for the species. The afternoon of human life must also have a significance of its own and cannot be merely a pitiful appendage to life's morning.

About the second half of life Jung went on to say that

Whoever carries over into the afternoon the law of the morning, or the natural aim, must pay for it with damage to his soul, just as surely as a growing youth who tries to carry over his childish egoism into adult life . . .

Following our earlier distinction, we may say that this peculiar "damage to our soul" wears two faces: self-regarding and other-regarding. When others treat us as mere objects rather than persons in our own right, then our dignity is damaged. But when we treat *ourselves* as a mere object–that is, as something frozen in the eyes of others (or of our own past)–then that treatment also does damage to our dignity. This is why Jung understood the psychological task of the second half of life to be precisely a process of individuation: "Become what you are" as the ancient Greek injunction put it.

In making these observations we come then to the polarity of *Individuation* versus *Objectification*, which constitutes a reaffirmation of the moral law defined by Kant: treat each person as an end in himself, never as a mere means. The same polarity is recapitulated in our interior mental life, when we treat ourselves as an "object" or as simply a self frozen in the past, in the case of those who try desperately to hold on to youth at any cost, which Simone de Beauvoir discusses critically in *The Coming of Age*. The result of this "inward objectification," suggests Jung, is damage to the soul and to dignity in old age.

In an ethical sense the ideal of dignity is frequently invoked in connection with the concept of "sanctity of life," implying unwavering commitment to the commandment "Thou shalt not kill." Pacifists understand this imperative in absolute terms, as forbidding war along with capital punishment or euthanasia. Current debates about end-of-life issues reflect this long and convoluted history with its roots in traditions of both religion and natural law ethics.

The recent debate about assisted suicide reminds that the traditional controversy over sanctity of life is very much alive.

The assisted suicide debate is timely because it invokes another basic polarity around the idea of dignity, the polarity between *Autonomy* and *Dependency*. Although Kant himself believed that "rational suicide was unethical, he also was the fountainhead of the Enlightenment ideal that equated human dignity with basic autonomy, or the capacity to set goals for oneself and choose the means to reach those goals. For most of our adult lives, we have some capacity to exercise autonomy in this basic sense. But there often comes a time, especially for the "oldest-old" (85+) when there is increased dependency on others, often for activities of daily living, sometimes for the most basic tasks of feeding, bathing and toileting. In these circumstances, the elderly person feels demeaned and undignified and may believe that the only way out is an exercise of autonomy to end life.

Judging from the very high suicide rates among the elderly, especially elderly men, there are groups in our society for whom dependency per se seems to entail a loss of dignity and the will to live. For example, it is not unusual to hear elderly people say they would rather die than go into a nursing home, or to ask a spouse to promise never to be placed in a nursing home. Before we agree too quickly that the "solution" to such conditions is an extended right to suicide, it would be wiser to examine whether there are ways to maintain the sense of dignity and hope among people in nursing homes, those nearing death, those with chronic illness, and those who are dependent in many other ways. I know of no better statement of the dialectic of autonomy and dependency than words from Florida Scott-Maxwell's *Measure of My Days*, a journal kept during her days as a nursing home resident:

> I had one fear. What if something went wrong, and I became an invalid? What if I became a burden, ceased to be a person and became a problem, a patient, someone who could not die?

> I was among people who could not die. How many longed to? Who should? Who can say? We cannot know what dying is. Is there a right moment for each of us? If we have hardly lived at all, it may be much harder to die. We may have to learn that we

failed to live our lives. Looking at the old from the outside I think–'Let them go, there is no one there. They have already gone and left their bodies behind. Make a law that is impossible to abuse, and allow release.' But inside the old, who makes the final decision? These are mysteries like everything else.

The profound ambivalence and sense of mystery reminds us that the simple polarity of autonomy versus dependency may very well be a false alternative. Instead of endorsing feelings of desperation ("Call Dr. Kevorkian!"), we would do better to challenge the underlying circumstances–for example, lack of pain management or substandard conditions of care–that lead a disturbing number of people to feel they are better off dead rather than living a life dependent on the care of others. What the entire debate about assisted suicide, and the deeper polarity of autonomy and dependency, needs above all is a sustained cultural and historical critique of the false choices and unexamined assumptions that limit our understanding of the issues. It is to that wider cultural and historical context that we turn now.

HISTORY AND CONTEMPORARY APPEAL OF THE IDEA OF DIGNITY

The basic formulation of human dignity goes back to the Latin phrase *dignitas hominis*, as used, for instance, by the Roman philosopher and statesman Cicero (Cicero, ed. Goold, 1975). But in Cicero's writings, we have two clearly distinguished views about what dignity is and where dignity comes from. First is the societal idea of dignity based on social role. Dignity in this respect refers to status or rank and above all to the concept of honor. Honor of course is traditionally an aristocratic idea. Modern societies also maintain this idea of dignity or honor, although now no longer applied to social class but instead to an office (rather than a person). Thus, for instance, we might refer to a member of Congress as "The Honorable . . ." or we speak of the need to maintain the office of the Presidency in high public respect.

Similarly, we routinely demand that citizens in a courtroom treat the judge with respect ("Your Honor"), on pain of being cited for contempt of court. In Cicero, this whole idea of honor or dignity is related to specific social role (as woman, public official, Roman citizen, and so on) and is therefore defined in different ways. Dignity in this first sense contains a multiplicity of meanings, as we saw in the second part of this chapter. On the other hand, there is also in Cicero an idea of dignity attached to universal human nature (Honecker, p. 260), which corresponds to the Stoic strand of his thought, to which we now turn.

The origins of the idea of human dignity in its universal sense go back to the Bible as well as Stoic philosophy with its concept of natural law. All of these ideas, which were to be profoundly influential in Western ethics, are overwhelmingly individualistic in their inspiration. It is an actual human individual, not an office or position, which bears the attribute of dignity. In that respect, these ideas of dignity and natural law differ markedly from the style of thinking, reflected, say, in Confucian sources where family solidarity or social role ("head of the family") are of incomparably greater importance.

In the modern Western civilization the ideal of human dignity has another history rooted in the liberal tradition of John Locke as later developed by Kant with his emphasis on rationality and autonomy. Kant formulates his ideal of human dignity in extremely formal or abstract terms: i.e., his Categorical Imperative demanding that humanity should never be used merely as a means but also as an end in itself. Interestingly, Kant ascribes human dignity only to rational beings, which means not to all members of the human species. For Kant, then, dignity follows from rationality, not from humanity as such. On this view, an infant would not possess a claim to dignity nor perhaps would a severely demented elderly person. We might treat such people in a dignified or respectful way, but only for the same reasons we treat dead bodies with a measure of respect: not because of a benefit we can directly confer (respect for another) but for other customary reasons (e . g., forming good habits, memory of previous qualities of character, etc.)

The Kantian ideals of autonomy and liberty tend to underscore negative rather than positive rights. According to the liberal tradition, these individual rights remain prior to any specific social structure or set of rules, which leads to problems addressed by the

idea of social contract. A social contract is set up in order to enforce
or safeguard these individual fundamental rights, an argument familiar in the context of the American Constitution. According to
liberal tradition, there is a societal responsibility to support the ideal
of human dignity.

This liberal tradition of thinking about rights and dignity is alive
and well in our own day: for example, in the theory of justice
elaborated by John Rawls. Rawls' requirement for moral principles
is that they should be quite general in form, universal in their
application, susceptible to adjudicate conflicting claims, and widely
recognized as a common standard for purposes of practical reasoning.

The contract tradition deriving from Kant and Rawls leaves
many questions open. What acts are incompatible with human dignity? Apparently torture, genocide, inflicting of atrocities, enslave-
ment and other forms of barbaric punishment are excluded. That
much seems clear. But soon enough questions become debatable.
For example, is capital punishment incompatible with human dignity? What about abortion? Or infanticide or euthanasia? Or does the
concept of human dignity actually *require* us to support the idea of
assisted suicide? These last examples show that moral consensus
about dignity is not easy to achieve.

Nonetheless, despite debate or ambiguity, the concept of "human
dignity" has assumed extraordinary importance in ethics and
constitutional law throughout the 20th century. For example, appeals to the language of "dignity" are found in the constitutions of
countries such as Canada, Germany, Greece, Ireland, Italy, Portugal, Spain, and Sweden. In U.S. Supreme Court decisions an appeal
to human dignity is constantly invoked. The Charter of the United
Nations, as well as other international documents such as the Universal Declaration of Human Rights, includes reference to "inherent dignity" connected to a notion of human rights cutting
across all cultural boundaries. Sometimes the idea of dignity refers
to the protection of life; at other times it denotes a broader ideal of
respect or quality of life.

Some have criticized "human dignity" as merely an empty rhetorical formula, a suspicion that the whole idea of dignity is obsolete, useless baggage. But in fact the history of the idea of dignity

shows two quite clear, though opposing meanings: first, an idea of intrinsic human nature created in the image of God; and, second, an idea of self-determination and subjectivity, reflected in the concept of autonomy. These two ideas about dignity are often in tension but their influence continues to be pervasive.

The German term for dignity or *"Menschenwurde"* has been at the center of the recent debate in bioethics in Europe (Birnbacher, 1983). In the context of debates around termination of life-sustaining treatment, an appeal to Menschenwurde often serves as a conversation stopper: a slogan that sets bounds for any further discussion. Birnbacher makes an observation very relevant to American society and the status of the elderly today: "The more pluralistic the values of a society become, and the more relativist its thinking about these values, the more it feels a need for taboo concepts defining, in a negative way, its residual identity." Other philosophers have agreed: "Human dignity seems to be one of the few common values in our world of philosophical pluralism" (Spiegelberg, 1983).

But is this idea of rock bottom "common values" actually correct? Or does rhetorical agreement point to a concept "a mile wide and an inch deep?" The appeal to rock bottom common values does not seem to hold true for America at the end of the 20th century. On the contrary, the more pluralistic and relativistic we now become—the post-modern tendency described earlier–the *less* convincing does any appeal to "human dignity" seem because there are fewer and fewer shared taboos of any kind. Some of the reasons for this collapse of taboos of all kinds are set forth by Philip Rieff in *The Triumph of the Therapeutic*. In the three decades since Rieff wrote that book, the therapeutic language of self-help has become all-pervasive in America. The language of mass media such as daytime TV or Internet chatrooms suggests that we have eroded all boundaries and collapsed all taboos, including the idea of "dignity," which does not seem much apparent on TV talk shows.

So we have a paradox. Appeals to dignity continue unceasingly through the 20th century, even at a time when the philosophical foundations of "common values" are less and less in evidence. The idea of dignity is easily dismissed as obsolete, and older people as a group seem less inclined than ever to appeal to ideas of dignity. Yet we find ourselves continuing to make appeals to dignity, especially when we imagine the ethical foundations of care of the aged. We cannot "locate" dignity as inherent in human beings in any obvious way, yet we also cannot get rid of the concept. What is the resolution of this paradox?

Martin Hailer and Dietrich Ritschl argue that

> Most useful and philosophically tenable seems to be the contention that Human Dignity is not automatically inherent in humans, as it were, but that it is imparted on others by speaking and acting. In other words, there has to be someone who tells me that I have Human Dignity, and by telling me and by acting in accordance with this pronouncement Human Dignity is imparted. (Hailer and Ritschl, p. 103)

They argue that the advantage of thinking of dignity as something "imparted" by a social relationship gives us a platform or basis on which to come to concrete decisions. But Hailer and Ritschl specifically exclude the possibility that such imparting of dignity could be left to arbitrary decisions of one person toward another. In sum, they develop instead a "social dimension of Human Dignity" construed as a *dialogical concept.* By this term they designate the agreement-character of society (or social contract), which is close to the line developed, in different ways, by John Rawls and Jurgen Habermas. Hailer and Ritschl want to exclude both an arbitrary situation ethics and at the same time eliminate an applied form of legalism with ever finer prescription of rules–a peculiar temptation to those who imagine that "better management" or an "improved code of ethics" will remedy any problems with dignity. They conclude that if ethics is to have "an anthropological basis, consisting of broader frame-references, [then] Human Dignity [is] one of them" (Hailer and Ritschl, p. 105).

What follows from this will be specific arguments that are well grounded and controlled: in short, that appeal to specific social circumstances, whether social policy for age-based entitlements or provision of services in long-term care. We cannot make progress in understanding the importance of dignity and aging unless we understand the specific logic and use of the concept of dignity to clarify obligations that arise in specific social circumstances. Only in those circumstances can we reconcile the polarities and make sense of the multiple meanings that dignity can have in old age.

For instance, what must interest us about the idea of human dignity, say, as applied to social services for the homebound will be questions about the character of formal services that either support or subvert dignity as something "imparted" by the transaction itself. Professionals and advocates for the aging commonly cite examples of acts that can subvert dignity: violating a person's privacy by witnessing nakedness; rendering care to incontinent persons; using a client's first name without first establishing a basis for such use; and so on.

These examples of "everyday ethics" may be more important than we think because they comprise the daily background conditions that give rise to mutual expectations: for instance, between patients and caregivers. If a person's dignity is eroded, not necessarily by a monumental assault but by the "tyranny of small decisions," then the result may be a person who feels unable to make claims, unable to complain, unworthy of being treated with dignity: in short, a vicious circle in which, for example, the slave no longer feels entitled to any status other than to be dependent and subject to others.

But the solution to cases of demeaning or dignity-diminishing acts is not as simple as it might seem. For example, just keeping people out of a nursing home may not be the answer. There is no question that the appeal of home care or assisted living is deeply rooted in the idea of retaining independence (i.e., dignity) and vast resources could be expended on behalf of that goal. It is not the purpose of this essay to argue against expanding community-based services for long-term care. But it seems doubtful that few of the current policy proposals for "alternatives to institutionalization" will, all by themselves, insure dignity for clients.

One problem with home care is that services are rendered by professionals or paraprofessionals in a setting that is, in Goffman's words, "off-stage." In our own home we are entitled to relax and be exempt from certain rules of self-presentation that might apply in quasi-public settings outside the home. We may also expect a degree of individualized treatment–for example, freedom from schedules and institutional regimen–which is supportive of dignity. But on the other hand, acts of disrespect and violations of dignity are more difficult to monitor or detect in home care settings than in institutions. The popular solution today is to insure dignity and individuality by means of the marketplace: that is, promote consumer direction of home care and long-term care decisions more generally, often on the analogy of younger disabled people.

The problem with promoting dignity through consumer sovereignty is that it cannot easily work for people with diminished mental capacity: e.g., failing memory, dementia, etc. Those with mental frailty are natural candidates for exploitation and scams of all kinds, as we see increasingly today in multibillion dollar levels of fraud, both in Medicare home care as well as in financial abuse and exploitation of the elderly. It would be a cruel irony if popular political appeals for deregulation and consumer sovereignty were to mask assaults on dignity that can take place through the marketplace as much as through bureaucracy.

Contemporary appeals to the marketplace and individual choice may sound as if they are based on the Kantian idea of autonomy or the transcendent value of the individual coming down to us from classical or Biblical sources. But that resemblance is an illusion. Contemporary marketplace individualism is a disguised ideology that masks the sources of power and prevents dialogue about who is best served by social constructions, including the marketplace itself. Markets, after all, are only a contingent social construct, not a transcendent source of meaning. The market is not "out there" in the world, any more than lines of latitude and longitude are painted on the earth. The dignity that people can maintain through consumer choice by itself reflects a very specific social role and sensibility: e.g., the feeling of self-respect that flows from "paying for the service oneself" rather than receiving "welfare."

The hunger for self-respect becomes more acute when other sources of strength begin to fail. But even power relationships, whether money or entitlements, that overcome the vulnerability of age can preserve their power only because people are willing to make claims and enforce demands based on collective ideals or agreements. Granted that dignity must be "imparted." It does not follow that it must only be imparted by money.

The opposing self-regarding and other-regarding dimensions of dignity are intertwined, as always, whether in the marketplace or in the bureaucracy. These arrangements are contingent; all arrangements are "up for grabs," as history teaches us over and over again. To insist upon the contingency of institutional structures is one way of locating dignity in the stream of history, and awareness of contingency helps remind us that "this too shall pass."

But awareness of contingency is not the same thing as post-modern relativism. The appeal to dignity, more strongly, the insistent *claim* to dignity, points to something in us which is genuinely transcendent, something which reflects our freedom to call into question all social roles, to say out loud that I am something more than my frailty or my role performances or my buying power. At that moment, the passive victim rises up to say "You can't treat me this way." The moment we speak those words, dialogue becomes possible and advocacy becomes inevitable. The outcome of the struggle is never certain, but this struggle for dignity emerges again and again through the course of history. It is a cry for justice as much as an affirmation of meaning. Which is why dignity in old age matters.

REFERENCES

Bayertz, K. (ed.). *Sanctity of Life and Human Dignity*, Kluwer: 1996.

Berger, P. "On the Obsolescence of the Concept of Honor," in *Invitation to Sociology*.

Birnbacher, D. "Ambiguities in the Concept of Menschenwurde," in Bayertz, pp. 107-121, 1966.

Christiansen, D. "Dignity in Aging: Notes on Geriatric Ethics." *Journal of Humanistic Psychology*, (Spring, 1978) 18:2, 41-54.

David, S.I. *With dignity: The Search for Medicare and Medicaid*. Westport, CT: Greenwood Press, 1985.

Fitzgerald, S. "Cost-effective Quality Alternative." *Assisted Living Today*, (Fall, 1995) 3:1, 1A+ (8 p.).

Frankl, V. "Facing the Transitoriness of Human Existence." *Generations*, (Fall, 1990) 14:4, 7-10.

Gross, M. "Dignity: The Keystone of Alzheimer's Care." *Nursing Homes*, (Sept., 1993) 42:7, 8-13.

Gutmann, D. "Strength or Stigma: The Aging Stranger." *Journal of Aging and Judaism*, (Winter, 1990) 5:2, 115-118.

Hailer, M. & Ritschl, D. "The General Notion of Human Dignity and The Specific Arguments in Medical Ethics," in Bayertz, *Sanctity of Life and Human Dignity*, pp. 91-106, 1966.

Hesse, K.A. "Ethical Issues and Terminal Management of the Old." *Journal of Geriatric Psychiatry*, (1995) 28:1, 75-95.

Heumann, L.F. & Boldy, D.P. (Eds.). *Aging in Place with Dignity: International Solutions Relating to the Low-Income and Frail Elderly*. Westport, CT: Praeger, 1993.

Holstein, M. "Normative Case: Chronological Age and Public Policy." *Generations*, (Fall, 1995) 19:3, 11-14.

Honecker, M. "On the Appeal for the Recognition of Human Dignity in Law and Morality," in Bayertz, *Sanctity of Life and Human Dignity*, pp. 257-273.

Jecker, N.S. "Physician-Assisted Death in the Netherlands and the United States: Ethical and Cultural Aspects of Health Policy Development." *Journal of the American Geriatrics Society*, (June, 1994) 42:6, 672-678.

Krause, D.R. "Institutional Living for the Elderly in Denmark: A Model for the United States." *Aging*, (Sept-Oct, 1981) 321-322.

Lasch, C. *The Culture of Narcissism*.

Lubove, R. *Struggle for Social Security, 1900-1935*. Pittsburgh: University of Pittsburgh Press, 1986.

Martin, S. & Smith, R.W. "OBRA Legislation and Recreational Activities: Enhancing Personal Control in Nursing Homes." *Activities, Adaptation and Aging*, (1993) 17:3, 1-14.

Miller, J.A. & K. Brown Wilson. "Concepts in Community Living: Assisted Living Program, Portland, Oregon," in Miller, Judith Ann, *Community-based Long-term Care: Innovative Models*. Newbury Park, CA: Sage Publications, 1991, 189-201.

Rein, J.E. "Preserving Dignity and Self-determination of the Elderly in the Face of Competing Interests and Grim Alternatives: A Proposal for Statutory Refocus and Reform." *George Washington Law Review*, (Aug., 1992) 60:6, 1818-1887.

Rieff, P. *The Triumph of the Therapeutic*.

Scheper, T.M.J.J. and Duursma, S.A. "Euthanasia: The Dutch Experience." *Age and Ageing*, (Jan., 1994) 23:1, 3-8.

Harvey, D. *The Condition of Postmodernity: An Equity into the Origins of Cultural Change*. Oxford: Blackwell, 1989.

Riley, M.W. & Riley, J.W., Jr. "Age Integration and the Lives of Older People." *The Gerontologist*, (Feb., 1994) 34:1, 110-115.

I. THE MEANING OF DIGNITY

Dignity and Quality of Life
in Old Age

Linda K. George, PhD

INTRODUCTION

I will begin this discussion of dignity and quality of life with an anecdote. This anecdote was told to me by my dear friend and cherished colleague, Elaine Brody, who has enjoyed a stellar career in aging research and practice. Elaine spent her career, as a social worker, at the Philadelphia Geriatric Center. Her participation in the worlds of both research and practice provided Elaine with a rich, first-hand view that permitted her to ground her work in the experiential context of late life.

Her anecdote concerns a very old woman, admitted to the Philadelphia Geriatric Center nursing home. This woman suffered from both advanced dementia and disabilities generated by physical illness. She was bed-and/or wheelchair-bound and had been unable to communicate verbally for some time. Her only behavioral problem,

[Haworth co-indexing entry note]: "Dignity and Quality of Life in Old Age." George, Linda K. Co-published simultaneously in *Journal of Gerontological Social Work* (The Haworth Press, Inc.) Vol. 29, No. 2/3, 1998, pp. 39-52; and: *Dignity and Old Age* (ed: Robert Disch, Rose Dobrof, and Harry R. Moody) The Haworth Press, Inc., 1998, pp. 39-52. Single or multiple copies of this article are available for a fee from The Haworth Document Delivery Service [1-800-342-9678, 9:00 a.m. - 5:00 p.m. (EST). E-mail address: getinfo@haworthpressinc.com].

beyond the obvious limitations posed by her medical conditions, was that she screamed without ceasing every time that she was given a bath. The staff were concerned about this woman's distress about being bathed. They talked to her family, who could offer no explanation for her behavior. They tried changing the temperature of the bath water, playing soft music, and talking to the woman in a soothing way. Nothing helped. Then, during one of her baths, a staff member came into the room to tell the nurse's aide something that she didn't want overheard by other patients. She closed the woman's door to share her information. As soon as the door closed, the older woman stopped screaming. From then on, so long as the door was closed, the woman accepted her bath with apparent tranquility. If the door was not closed, however, she screamed until the bath was over and she was dressed.

This anecdote is telling for two reasons. First, it challenges our assumptions about what persons suffering from advanced dementia can understand. More importantly for our purposes, this anecdote seems related to both a sense of dignity and quality of life. It suggests that, even in conditions of severe mental and physical impairment, people can treasure a sense of dignity and suffer if their dignity is violated.

Given this introduction, the remainder of my comments will focus on three issues related to the connections between dignity and quality of life. First, I will briefly discuss definitional issues. Hopefully, this will not be an exercise in semantics—but rather will lay the foundation for a shared sense of what dignity and quality of life mean for the purposes of this discussion. Second, I will discuss the links that I see between dignity and quality of life. These comments will include my view of how previous research has informed our understanding of dignity despite the fact that the term "dignity" has not been explicitly used in that research. Finally, I will posit that one of the most interesting facets of both quality of life and dignity is their dialectical character as both personal and social phenomena.

DEFINITIONAL ISSUES

Traditional dictionaries typically are not useful references for understanding terms as they are used in research and practice. Because one of the challenges of the social sciences is to explicate the links between scientific or professional concepts and everyday life experience, however, it can be valuable to keep in mind conventional, as well as scientific, meanings. That is especially true in cases such as this, in which we are interested in a concept, such as dignity, that has not been used scientifically (at least in the social sciences).

The dictionary in my office, an abridged version of Webster's (1965, p. 233), lists three meanings for dignity:

1. "the quality or state of being worthy, honored, or esteemed,"
2. "a high rank, honor, or position," and
3. "formal reserve of manner or language."

For our purposes, the first definition is most relevant. Indeed, it expresses well the way that we usually think about dignity in nonscientific terms.

Although this definition is meaningful for our purposes, the dictionary tells us little about how dignity occurs in the world. Is it rare or common? What determines this "quality or state?" What are its consequences? For my purposes, more specifically, how is dignity related to well-being and quality of life?

In contrast to dignity, the term "quality of life" has a long tradition in the study of aging, although its meaning remains fluid and has not yet become standardized. My own thinking about well-being or quality of life has evolved considerably over time. In 1980, I co-authored a book titled, *Quality of Life for Older Persons* (George & Bearon, 1980). To my knowledge, this was the first book in aging to focus on quality of life–and certainly it was among the first. At that time, I defined quality of life as characterized by two conditions: first, the individual meets the demands of the environment; and second, the individual perceives and experiences a sense of general well-being. Using this definition, quality of life is compromised when the individual cannot meet the level of environmental demands he or she confronts, or can do so only at the cost of personal well-being. Quality of life, I argued, has both objective and subjective components. The degree to which the individual meets the demands of the environment is an objective phenomenon, whereas perceptions of well-being are subjective.

After nearly 20 years of research and study, I believe that my initial definition of quality of life was overly restrictive. Specifically, I am now convinced that one can have high quality of life, even if one is unable meet the demands of the environment. To take my original definition seriously to its logical limits could lead to the conclusion that people who are physically or mentally disabled, or otherwise incapable of independent self-care, are precluded from experiencing high quality of life. If there is one lesson that I have learned in the past 20 years, it is that the human spirit has the capacity to thrive in conditions that most of us would consider traumatic or distasteful, as well as those that are comfortable and gratifying. Certainly, many people cannot thrive emotionally–and, although the environment clearly affects the likelihood that one will perceive life to be of high quality, mismatches occur in both directions. That is, there are people who define their lives as miserable despite capacities far beyond those needed to meet environmental demands as well as people who seem to find life rewarding despite the fact that they cannot meet the environmental demands necessary for independent living.

A natural corollary to my evolving view of quality of life has been an emphasis in my research on the relationships among *objective demands* of the environment and capacities of the individual, on the one hand, and *subjective perceptions* of life quality on the other hand. That is, rather than examine quality of life as having both objective and subjective requirements, my more recent work focuses on (1) the conditions under which perceived quality of life remains high despite unfavorable environments and/or capacities and (2) the social and psychological processes that seem to be more important determinants of perceived quality of life than objective conditions.

A note of caution is probably prudent at this point. Environmental conditions and personal capacities are clearly important for perceived quality of life. Persons who have reasonable health, adequate incomes, and supportive relationships with family and friends are more likely to perceive life quality as high than those without such objective resources (e.g., Campbell, Converse, & Rodgers, 1976; George, Okun, & Landerman, 1985; Liang, Dvorkin, Kahana, & Mazian, 1980; Strain & Chappell, 1982). Therefore, I favor policies and programs that transfer resources to societal members who lack

them and that help people to compensate for immutable deprivations. But, as a scholar, I don't find the predictable relationships
between material or social assets and well-being as interesting as
the condition under which objective conditions have little importance for life quality. I think that we learn more about other people
when we observe them under stress than when all is going well for
them. Similarly, I think that we learn more about the human spirit
when we study people facing challenges to well-being than people
who do not face such challenges.

DIGNITY AND QUALITY OF LIFE: CLUES FROM PREVIOUS RESEARCH

As noted previously, social and behavioral research has not, to
my knowledge, focused directly on dignity. There is, however, a
broad range of relevant research on what I call "social psychological resources." In general, my research and that of many other
scholars suggests that social psychological resources such as self-
esteem, autonomy, a sense of control, and self-direction are major
factors in perceptions of high life quality (e.g., Holahan & Holahan,
1987; McCrae & Costa, 1983; Ward, Sherman, & LaGory, 1984). In
part, these resources explain *why* objective capacities and environmental factors are robustly related to perceptions of well-being.
Health, economic assets, and strong social ties are important to life
quality in large part because they provide us with strong and rewarding identities, validate our sense of self-worth, and help us feel
that we have a significant degree of control over the directions that
our lives take. Indeed, the strongest evidence of the importance of
social psychological resources is their established role in mediating
between the objective conditions of our lives and our subjective
experience of life (e.g., Carp & Carp, 1982; Krause, 1987; Norris &
Murrell, 1984).

In addition, research suggests that some people are able to sustain
strong social identities, feelings of self-worth, and a sense of control
even when objective life circumstances are highly unfavorable
(e.g., Breytspraak, 1984; Whitbourne, 1987). In these instances, the
social psychological resources themselves appear sufficient for gen-
erating perceptions of life quality. Thus, social psychological re-

sources can have a direct impact on perceptions of well-being, obviating the individual's reliance upon external circumstances for experiencing high quality of life. Conversely, individuals whose social psychological resources are deficient typically describe their life quality as poor, regardless of their objective capacities and environmental demands and resources. An obvious priority topic for future research in this field is to determine how it is that some people can sustain higher levels of identity, self-worth, and sense of autonomy in the absence of external material or social reinforcement.

Obviously, I cannot discuss the link between dignity and quality of life on the basis of empirical research. But I can attempt to make conceptual and interpretive links between the two phenomena, based in part on previous research on related issues. I do not think that dignity is a social psychological resource of the same type as self-esteem, social identity, and a sense of control. Instead, I believe that there are intangible characteristics of the social environment that operate in much the same way as objective capacities and material resources–that is, as robust predictors of social psychological resources. I would hypothesize that dignity is, in fact, a characteristic of the social environment–it is not material in the ways that health and economic resources are, but it is one of a number of parameters of social context that differ across environments and have potentially important direct effects on perceived life quality. Dignity also, undoubtedly, has consequential indirect effects on life quality as well, via its impact on social psychological resources. As an aside, other candidates for parameters of the social environment worth examining in future research include degree of predictability, stability, and latitude for discretionary behavior.

Before turning to the final section of comments, I'd like to pass along an interesting conversation that I had about the concept of dignity. One of my close friends is an attorney; I mentioned this issue to her. She offered an interesting observation. In North Carolina civil law, including domestic law, damages may be sought for a category of behaviors termed "indignities." In terms of severity, indignities are assumed to be less damaging than physical assault or damage to professional reputation. But they are eligible for both actual and punitive damages. The kinds of behaviors viewed as legal indignities are broad and heterogeneous, including everything from public humiliation to name-calling in private. Because of the breadth and vagueness of the term, lawyers are often reluctant to file suits based solely on indignities. But this attorney indicated that indignities are often important elements in many other kinds of suits ranging from libel/slander to divorce to inheritance squabbles. She also reported that judges often use evidence of indignities to adjust up or down monetary damages, property settlements in divorces, and even decisions in child custody suits. Whether lawyers find the notion of indignities useful or not, the fact that they have legal status in some states reinforces several points I've tried to make: dignity (or the lack thereof) is demonstrable, it is consequential, and it is a mutable characteristic of social environments and interactions.

DIGNITY: THE DIALECTIC OF PERSONAL AND SOCIAL FOUNDATIONS

I am often asked whether the types of phenomena I frequently study—phenomena such as self-worth and perceived quality of life—are personal or social in nature. This is a difficult and, I believe, ultimately inappropriate question. Social-psychological states such as identity and life satisfaction are a complex combination of the personal and the social or interpersonal. Indeed, I am attracted to the study of such phenomena precisely because of their dual natures as both highly personal and, usually, socially-developed and sustained.

The term dialectic has been used in multiple ways. One of its conventional definitions is reasoning that juxtaposes opposed or contradictory ideas and seeks to resolve their conflict by synthesis or logic. Phenomena such as self-esteem and a sense of autonomy are dialectical in that they represent complex intersections of the psychological and the social. I will argue that dignity is dialectical in the same fashion. Let's consider three apparent polarities with regard to dignity. I hope to convince you that these are, in fact, opposite sides of the same coin.

Is Dignity Bestowed or Claimed? One possible polarity is whether dignity is bestowed upon individuals by others or whether it exists because individuals claim it. Some people appear to view dignity as a state of esteem or honor that cannot be experienced unless members of the social environment treat others in a way that conveys dignity. Other people might argue that dignity is a personal resource–regardless of the reactions or assumptions of other people, no one can take away one's fundamental dignity.

Closely related to this issue is whether dignity is, can be, or should be earned. We have probably all heard comments to the effect that "I will give him/her dignity and respect when he/she earns it." This philosophy views dignity as conditional upon the behaviors and/or attitudes of individuals. It is a variant of the view that dignity is bestowed by others. But this view ignores the *origins* of dignity. I am aware of no research on the origins of self-dignity. Nonetheless, it seems certain that self-dignity develops during so-cialization–as do other psychosocial resources (e.g., self-esteem, a sense of mastery) (e.g., Breytspraak, 1984). Undoubtedly, one's sense of dignity can be modified throughout life as a result of experience. But it is unlikely that individuals can develop a sense of self-dignity unless others bestow it freely rather than requiring that it be earned. If one receives dignity unconditionally from others, one is likely to bestow dignity on others as well, regardless of their personal characteristics or behaviors. Thus, developing a sense of self-dignity and treating others with dignity would seem to go hand-in-hand. Indeed, self-dignity functions not only to increase our willingness to treat others with dignity, but also to stake a claim that we be treated with dignity by others.

The argument that I am making here is that the view that dignity is something to be earned fails on logical grounds. How can one develop a sense of self-dignity, which can then be used as a claim to being treated with dignity by others, if it must be earned? There is a "catch-22" quality to phenomena such as dignity if others won't give it to you unless you have it and you can't have it in the first place if others won't give it to you.

At any rate, I would argue that dignity is both bestowed by others in the immediate social environment and exists independently of it. Self-dignity would seem to be a component of quality of life. It is difficult to imagine high life quality without a fundamental sense of self-dignity. But I'm confident that the probability of high quality of life is greatest when the personal and the social act in concert–that is, when individuals have a sense of self-dignity and members of the social environment convey the message that one is deserving of dignity.

Is Dignity a Necessity or a Luxury? Duke University, my employer, recently held a session for non-faculty personnel intended primarily, so far as I can tell, to boost morale. The content of the session focused on the general theme of "you are important to us and we value your contributions." When two of my employees, who were *required* to attend the session, returned and I asked them if they liked it, one snapped "If they want to show me that I'm important to them, they should take the money they spend on those kind of things and use it to give me a bigger raise." The other employee agreed, stating that the session had been "a waste of time" and that its major effect was to put her behind in getting her work done that day. One way of interpreting this experience is to view the administration's motives as the desire to reinforce a sense of dignity and worth toward its employees, with the latter apparently unimpressed by those motives. For me this scenario is related to the question of whether dignity is a necessity for functional social systems or whether it is a luxury–nice to have, but no substitute for more basic requirements. We might ask ourselves this question with regard to our older population, especially that portion of it that is impaired and dependent on others. If, as a society, we meet the physical, medical, and economic needs of impaired older adults, do we need to treat them with dignity too?

Again, I think that strong cases can be made for both sides of this issue, but that the wisest course is to recognize that both are valid. From the point of view of simple survival, being treated with dignity is undoubtedly a luxury. One can survive without it–and the termination of basic life necessities could threaten existence in a way that the absence of dignity could not. From the perspective of quality of life, however, it is my belief that a fundamental sense of dignity–both self-dignity and as bestowed by others–is a necessity rather than a luxury. Thus, to the extent that we wish to make quality of life–rather than quantity of life or the mere existence of life–an explicit goal, we must incorporate attention to the more intangible facets of existence, including dignity.

One of the toughest audiences for me in this regard has been policy makers who face what are, in my career, unprecedented limits on resources in proportion to needs. I often get the sense from these weary warriors that they are so consumed and overwhelmed by the challenges of meeting the physical and economic needs of our most needy older adults that more subjective issues of life quality are simply, by definition, considered outside of their purview. And yet, increasing the degree to which clinicians and service providers treat their patients with dignity and respect is potentially an extraordinarily inexpensive way of bolstering life quality. We should not have to pay more for services that are delivered in an atmosphere of dignity and respect than for those that elicit feelings of dependency and devaluation. To return to the anecdote with which I started these comments, can it really cost much more to have nurse's aides who close bedroom doors when undressing and bathing a patient than to have those who won't?

Note that I said that social environments that include an atmosphere of dignity are *potentially* inexpensive ways of increasing quality of life. In reality, of course, the cost of such environments will depend upon the steps taken to insure that older adults (everyone, for that matter) are treated with dignity. I turn to that issue next. But to summarize this issue, it seems to me that whether dignity is viewed as a necessity or a luxury depends upon the criterion we use–for mere survival, it is a luxury; for quality of life, it is probably a necessity.

Can Dignity Be Legislated? If there is substantial consensus that dignity should characterize interactions in our society, including interactions between impaired older adults and their service providers, a key practical question consequent to this conclusion is: Can we legislate or regulate such behavior? Or, is dignity so subjective and amorphous that we cannot hope to develop and enforce regulations requiring it? In the latter case, we can only hope that people will voluntarily choose to treat others with dignity.

Again, I believe that valid arguments can be made on both sides of this issue–or, more accurately, that dignity can be legislated at certain levels, but not at others. Our society has a long history of legislation intended to prohibit some behaviors and to encourage the development of other behaviors and attitudes that will be more far-reaching than what can be objectively and routinely enforced. Anti-discrimination legislation of all kinds falls under this umbrella, for example. Legislation can be targeted at severe violations of dignity, as laws in some states that prohibit "indignities" demonstrate. Although legislation can probably be targeted toward only relatively serious breaches of dignity, at least some behaviors can be regulated. With regard to less severe, but potentially consequential forms of indignity, intervention can probably best be targeted at specific social environments. Nursing homes, rest homes, and hospitals, for example, can implement regulations to protect resident and patient privacy and, to the extent possible, autonomy. Employees of all kinds of organizations can have their raises and promotions based, in part, on their demeanor in general and their respect for the dignity of others in particular. Thus, legislation, regulation, and material incentives can be used to prohibit behaviors that exceed the limits of human dignity and to encourage and reward more subtle forms of dignity.

Ultimately, however, dignity is voluntary, especially the forms that can make a critical difference between survival and quality of life. True quality of life rests on a foundation that goes beyond the easily measurable and enforceable. It is dependent on a social contract that specifies how behavior is enacted, as well as on what behaviors occur. Quality of life depends not only on the occurrence of some behaviors, but also on the suppression of others. Several authors who write for the educated public as well as professionals have recently focused attention on what they perceive as the demise of *civility* in our society–and its dehumanizing consequences (e.g., Bellah, Marsden, Sullivan, Swidler, & Tipton, 1985; Peck, 1993). They warn that our preferences for the informal and casual, rather than the formal and constrained, have had a presumably unintended consequence of eroding basic politeness, respect for others–and, perhaps, self-respect. Their suggestions for correcting this dysfunctional trend are not to legislate or regulate behavior, but simply for us, as thoughtful human beings, to demand better of ourselves and others. In many ways, I agree with this conclusion. In the final analysis, dignity can best be given voluntarily, representing a commitment to others that exceeds any that can be legislated.

Special issues come to mind when considering dignity as experienced by dependent or disabled older adults. It requires considerable time, energy, and other resources to use the courts to enforce legislative prohibitions on indignities. It is unlikely that most of us would choose to use our limited resources to pursue justice for indignities. We would either put up with them or seek new social environments where indignities are less likely to occur. It is even less likely that impaired older adults will be able to seek justice for indignities through the courts–most simply could not, even if they wished to do so. In addition, impaired older adults often cannot take the step of switching environments–or changing the environments in which they live. Thus, not only are dependent and disabled people less likely to use regulations and legislation to protect their dignity, they also are less likely to be able to avoid such treatment.

In addition to having fewer resources and less power to change their environments, there is reason to believe that dependent and disabled persons are more likely to be harmed by dehumanizing environments. This view is compatible with *environmental press theory*, developed and empirically supported by Lawton and colleagues (Lawton, 1982; Lawton & Nahemow, 1973). This theory postulates that as physical, mental, and social capacities become impaired, people can tolerate (and thrive, should we ever come to view this as a realistic goal for impaired older adults) in increasingly narrow and more supportive environments. That is, the more impaired and dependent people are, the more sensitive they are to both beneficial and harmful characteristics of their environments.

Given that the surest way to protect dignity is to have individuals voluntarily treat themselves and others with dignity, a natural question arises: Can we teach people to treat others with dignity? I think that the answer is a conditional "yes." I believe that we can sensitize people to issues of dignity and, in doing so, increase the likelihood of their treating others as deserving dignity. Lack of dignity probably reflects indifference or ignorance, more often than malevolence. Referring back to the anecdote at the beginning of my comments, the nurses aides were concerned about why their patient became hysterical when bathed–and, when they discovered the reason for the screams, they changed their behavior to make the patient more comfortable. One might argue that, if the aides had respected the dignity of the patient from the outset, the problem would never have occurred–but I think that a gentler view is more appropriate. Dignity is one of multiple issues that we must attend to in our interactions in the social world. I believe that simply "raising our consciousness" about it, to use a phrase of the 1960's, can help to overcome the indifference and ignorance that stands in the way of dignity. Hopefully training sessions designed to sensitize people to dignity–and conferences such as this one–can help to increase the prevalence of dignity in human interactions.

CONCLUSION

This volume addresses an issue that is, by definition, as much subjective as objective; that is more intangible than tangible. After nearly 20 years of research, I am firmly convinced that quality of life is based as much–and sometimes more–on the subjective and intangible as the objective and tangible. It is especially important that dignity and related issues receive attention in efforts to serve the dependent and disabled because they have little opportunity to change environments and, yet, may be more sensitive to environmental conditions. Many people who experience severe economic, physical, and social deprivations nonetheless experience high quality of life–specifically by focusing on the subjective and intangible. If our most needy citizens are willing to claim high quality of life, *despite* rather than *because* of objective life circumstances, we must do our part to help them to age with dignity.

REFERENCES

Bellah, R., Marsden, P., Sullivan, W., Swidler, A., & Tipton, S. (1985). *Habits of the Heart*. Berkeley: University of California Press.

Breytspraak, L.M. (1984). *The Development of Self in Later Life*. Boston: Little, Brown.

Campbell, A., Converse, P.E., & Rodgers, W.L. (1976). *The Quality of American Life*. New York: Russell Sage Foundation.

Carp, F.M. & Carp, A. (1982). Test of a model of domain satisfactions and well-being: Equity considerations. *Research on Aging, 4,* 503-522.

George, L.K. & Bearon, L.B. (1980). *Quality of Life in Older Persons: Meaning and Measurement*. New York: Human Sciences Press.

George, L.K., Okun, M.A., & Landerman, R. (1985). Age as a moderator of the determinants of life satisfaction. *Research on Aging, 7,* 209-233.

Holahan, C.K. & Holahan, C.J. (1987). Self-efficacy, social support, and depression in aging: A longitudinal analysis. *Journal of Gerontology, 42,* 65-68.

Krause, N. (1987). Chronic strain, locus of control, and distress in older adults. *Psychology and Aging, 2,* 375-382,

Lawton, M.P. (1982). Competence, environmental press, and the adaptation of older people. In M.P. Lawton, P.G. Windley, & T.O. Byerts (eds.), *Aging and the Environment: Theoretical Approaches* (pp. 33-59). New York: Springer.

Lawton, M.P. & Nahemow, L. (1973). Ecology and the aging process. In C. Eisdorfer & M.P. Lawton (eds.), *Psychology of Adult Development and Aging* (pp. 619-674). Washington, DC: American Psychological Association.

Liang, J., Dvorkin, L., Kahana, E., & Mazian, F. (1980). Social integration and morale: A re-examination. *Journal of Gerontology, 35,* 746-757.

McCrae, R.R. & Costa, P.T., Jr. (1983). Psychological maturity and subjective well-being: Toward a new synthesis. *Developmental Psychology, 19,* 243-248.

Norris, F.H. & Murrell, S.A. (1984). Protective function of resources related to life events, global stress, and depression in older adults. *Journal of Health and Social Behavior, 25,* 424-437.

Peck, M.S. (1993). *A World Waiting To Be Born: Civility Rediscovered.* New York: Bantam Books.

Strain, L.A. & Chappell, N.L. (1982). Confidants: Do they make a difference in quality of life? *Research on Aging, 4,* 479-502.

Ward, R.A., Sherman, S.R., & LaGory, M. (1984). Subjective network assessments and subjective well-being. *Journal of Gerontology, 39,* 93-101.

Webster's Seventh New Collegiate Dictionary (1965). Springfield, MA: G. & C. Merriam Company.

Whitbourne, S.K. (1987). Personality development in adulthood and old age: Relationships among identity style, health, and well-being. *Annual Review of Gerontology and Geriatrics, 7,* 189-216.

Respecting Ethnic Elders:
A Perspective for Care Providers

Jo Ann Damron-Rodriguez, PhD

INTRODUCTION

Can professionals provide care to older persons in ways that respect, not diminish, their dignity? To do this calls for an appreciation of the elder's strengths won from a life lived, as well as an assessment of late life frailties. Additionally, it requires an appreciation of the great diversity of the older population (Yee & Gelfand, 1992).

The older minority population is growing at a more rapid rate than the majority elderly population (American Association of Retired Persons, 1989). From 1970 to 1995 African American elderly increased 40%, Asian American 109% and Hispanic American elderly increased 98% (Valle, 1989; AARP, 1988). Diversity for all older persons is based not only on ethnicity but on gender, age, health status/functioning and socioeconomic status as well.

In order to develop a perspective for respectful care provision with attention to the breadth of these issues, key concepts which will help us to understand ethnic aging will be defined. These concepts will then be translated into a practice perspective and service relevant considerations for care providers.

[Haworth co-indexing entry note]: "Respecting Ethnic Elders: A Perspective for Care Providers." Damron-Rodriguez, Jo Ann. Co-published simultaneously in *Journal of Gerontological Social Work* (The Haworth Press, Inc.) Vol. 29, No. 2/3, 1998, pp. 53-72; and: *Dignity and Old Age* (ed: Robert Disch, Rose Dobrof, and Harry R. Moody) The Haworth Press, Inc., 1998, pp. 53-72. Single or multiple copies of this article are available for a fee from The Haworth Document Delivery Service [1-800-342-9678, 9:00 a.m. - 5:00 p.m. (EST). E-mail address: getinfo@haworthpressinc.com].

DIGNITY AND RESPECT:
AN INTERACTIONAL PERSPECTIVE

The definitions of dignity and respect set the foundation for understanding the interactional nature of respectful care. Dignity comes from the Latin *dignities* meaning worth, merit, or *dingus*, worthy (Neufeldt & Guralnik, 1991). Thus, dignity is defined as the quality of being worthy of esteem or honor; worthiness. In its smallest sense dignity means loftiness of appearance but in the larger sense it means proper pride and self-respect. Dignity is then an inner quality which arises and is maintained by the individual in interaction with her/his world. In late life care providers can make significant contributions or diminutions to the maintenance of the dignity of the older person. However, older persons themselves are the source of dignity.

Respect comes from the Latin *respectus* to look at, to look back on (Neufeldt & Guralnik, 1991). To respect is to feel or show honor or esteem for, hold in high regard or to show consideration for. Respect also admonishes us to avoid intruding upon or interfering with the respected one. In its least shallow sense and yet its most cliched form, "respect your elders" means only deference or dutiful regard. In its deepest sense respect means to attend to another honoring their worth and their separateness.

It is not the job of service providers to dignify or "to give dignity to, to make seem worthy or noble" as in a false sense of awarding dignity to another. Rather, it is the service provider's, health care professional's and clergy's role to respect the intrinsic dignity residing in the individual. Use of the term elder denotes this respect. Elder is defined as "one having authority by virtue of age and experience" (Neufeldt & Guralnik, 1991). Ethnic elder appropriately connotes the respect given to older persons within many ethnic and cultural groups (Gelfand & Yee, 1992).

AGING, DIGNITY AND INTEGRITY:
A LIFECOURSE PERSPECTIVE

To find one's life worthy of respect is defined by Erikson (1963) as the distinctive virtue of late life, "ego integrity." His eloquent description as follows provides a theme for this discourse:

Although aware of the relativity of all the various life styles which have given meaning to human striving, the possessor of integrity is ready to defend the *dignity* of his own life style against all physical and economic threats. For he knows that an individual life is the accidental coincidence of but one life cycle with but one segment of history; and that for him all human integrity stands or falls with the one style of integrity of which he partakes. (Erikson, 263-269)

In Erikson's view a life is the person's "one and only adventure in history." An older adult who possesses ego integrity accepts the good and the bad of their life events as contributing to the creation of who he or she has become. Erikson emphasized that this meant "the acceptance of one's one and only life cycle as something that had to be and that, by necessity, permitted of no substitutions" (1963: 263-269). In contrast, for those who enter late life in despair the focus is on the life not lived, a sense of having abandoned their own life.

In either case Erikson's perspective is one of the life course. From this perspective, the end of life must be seen as connected with the whole of life. This life course perspective broadens our view of aging by including personal biographies, cultural factors, and sociohistorical context (Stoller & Gibson, 1997). Integrity and dignity are actualized by the individual but in interaction with others. Erikson as a social psychologist views human development as an interactive process between the individual and the significant others who person his/her social world. In late life, care providers are often a significant part of this social world.

Two more recent works add to the Eriksonian perspective of late life development and relate to ethnic aging. Kaufman (1986) finds themes in older adult's lives which create an "ageless self." Bateson (1990) describes women's work of "composing a life" through improvising with the materials allocated to them. She emphasizes the discontinuities or transitions as particularly significant in defining a life. Both the continuities and the transitions for ethnic elders may be ways to understand how they have built a life with what they have taken from their culture of origin and has been presented to them in their country of residence.

This cultural and ethnic identity is particularly rich background for late life self-respect and pride. It relates the individual life to the life of the group as it continues over time. In the cultural perspective the individual history interfaces with cultural events shared by a people. Developmentally cultural heritage and ethnicity can be adaptive resources for elders in reaching a sense of wholeness with the past and well-being in the present which is the essence of integrity.

If our environments for children are designed to facilitate their growth at each particular stage of development, then should not our environments for elders provide opportunities for them to accomplish late life developmental tasks such as the development of integrity over the life course (Damron-Rodriguez, 1991)? Instead it could be asserted that many care environments for elders are designed for childlike activities, e.g., coloring, simple crafts.

The professional's assessment of the patient, though decidedly not a life review, should include major life transitions and social roles. Long term care settings could incorporate recognition of the importance of historical events, and past individual accomplishment through the display of photographs, posting of bio-sketches, gathering of reminisce groups and taking oral histories. In addition to present tense activities, incorporating life review as a real developmental task respects the elder's process rather than discarding the developmental work as "dwelling in the past."

AGING AND ETHNICITY

An important aspect of what Erikson describes as "the dignity of his/her own life style" is cultural and ethnic identity. Ethnic identification based on race, religion, or national origin distinguishes individuals with a group membership classified by their degree of affiliation (Cox, 1993). Hollsberg (1982) distinguishes a criteria of ethnicity as its sense of peoplehood with a shared history. Cultural elements related to ethnic identification are distinct values, beliefs, language, and religion (Gelfand, 1994). These cultural elements may be woven into the fabric of individual integrity. The transitions of the life course for ethnic elders may have been modified significantly by need to take on responsibilities of adulthood early and aborting their childhood (Barresi, 1987). These can influence the aging experience and definitions of health and dependence in late life (Gelfand, 1994).

The importance of religion in the lives of older persons relates to their ethnic identity (Chatters & Taylor, 1994; Levin, Markides & Ray, 1996). Judaism is an example of how religion may be a primary ethnic identification which is the core of the sense of peoplehood (Gelfand, 1994). Religion is historically an integral component of the social support system of ethnic elders as documented for African Americans (Chatters & Taylor, 1994).

The Cross-Cultural Exchange of Provider and Elder

Health professionals and other care providers also bring cultural and ethnic identity to the process of care provision (Grant & Finocchio, 1995). Thus, it is a cross-cultural exchange to give and receive assistance. Generational, as well as ethnic, differences add to the complexity of accomplishing elder care based in respect (Gelfand, 1994).

For both clients and professionals, culture is part of determining what they see as a health problem. What a symptom is and what it means and what to do about it is a judgement call and each analysis will be based on past experience as well as current options. For ethnic elders this analysis is often done with the assistance of family or other members of their support system who hold similar views. For elders, most beliefs about health and illness come from everyday experiences and most health care occurs at home. In a diverse population health and service decisions are made using widely varying criteria.

Biomedical health care providers have a specialist culture viewpoint driven from orientations, expectations and organization of Western (America) society (Barker, 1994). This contrasts with the generalist viewpoint held by many patients, especially the elderly and non-Western groups. She points to incongruities that may arise in relation to the basic life trajectory, the meaning of health, family roles, dependence and notions of time.

Examples are the general beliefs of forces that contribute to ill health by creating imbalance such as the Chinese expansion and contraction or some groups in Mexico that speak of hot and cold.

Chinese elders may use foods to control equilibrium (Chau et al., 1990). To address these causal factors for health problems traditional folk remedies such as herbal teas may be used.

A recent study (Frank et al., 1995) examined the meaning of late life health for Eastern-Euro-American, African-American, Chinese-American and Hispanic-American community-dwelling older persons. Although many had been living in the U.S. for years, most were immigrants. The definitions of the meaning of health in late life that emerged from the focus groups for all ethnic groups encompassed physical, psychological, spiritual, and social aspects. There were marked similarities, related to defining health in late life, as well as ethnic group differences. The following quotes by ethnic elders illustrate the differences.

> *Chinese-American Elder*: I'm up there in age and my heart is content at this age. I realize that at this age, if I didn't have my mind and my health I would not be happy. The most important thing is being content. The mind and the body work together and must be in balance. If your heart is not good then it will affect your physical health. Don't be too serious about your life.

> *European-American Elder*: Being healthy means that you can go on, get up in the morning, do what you need to do to take care of yourself then go out and meet people, be among organizations and activities.

The emphasis on activity, to some degree present in all groups, was emphasized most in the Eastern-Euro-American group. The definitions of health embraced by the European-Americans in this research may more closely reflect the values of the planners of senior activities at senior centers than values of non-western older adults.

Professionals based in a Western perspective are more likely to talk about the specific virus and how to kill it. Aspects relevant to this health professionals' culture are: cure rather than palliation, returning the patient to productivity as soon as possible, constant monitoring and alteration of treatment, technology, and strict controls on who will provide treatment (Barker, 1994). These relate in many ways to the difference in the nature of informal or personal care giving and formal or professional roles as described by Litwak (1985).

Facilitating cross-cultural communication is based in understanding both worldviews and negotiating any miscommunications. Culturally congruent care involves interventions that are acceptable to the consumer and appropriate for the provider (Kavanagh & Kennedy, 1992). To reach cultural congruence the older adult's original perspective must be accommodated, negotiated with the provider, or the provider or client must restructure their beliefs. Berlin and Fowkes (1983) present the LEARN model to accomplish the necessary negotiations between provider and ethnic class. The LEARN model consists of the following steps: (1) Listen with sympathy to patients explanations; (2) Explain your perceptions; (3) Acknowledge and discuss differences; (4) Recommend treatment or service and (5) Negotiate agreement.

DIVERSITY AND ETHNICITY

Erikson calls us to recognize diversity by appreciating that each person must understand the "relativity of all the various life styles" while being prepared to "defend the *dignity* of his own life style." Diversity is related not only to differences between ethnic groups but within ethnic groups. Ethnicity has relative value based on a variety of factors. Each individual ethnic elder brings a unique combination of a myriad of factors to create their life.

Clearly one important factor in diversity of ethnic elders is country of origin. Hispanic American elders may identify as Mexican American, Puerto Rican American, Cuban American, Spanish American or from one of any of the Central and South American countries. Asian and Pacific Islander Americans are composed of 22 distinct ethnic groupings. Urban versus rural differences for African American older persons may have significant cultural implications. European American elders will vary greatly based on generation in this country and other distinguishing factors in the degree of assimilation or ethnic identification. Ethnic elders also vary based on generation in this country, cohort, religion, language, and socioeconomic status. Ethnic differences also relate to immigration status and pattern, including age of immigration. The family pattern of migration is important, whether the elder came first alone, later after others were economically established or if he/she was brought to this country for elder care.

Gender is another major aspect of difference in aging process and also relates to ethnicity (Dressel, 1988). Men and women both biologically and socially experience age in significantly different ways. Further gender roles may be more firmly delineated among ethnic elders than among the broader culture and than among subsequent generations of their own culture. Barker (1992) urges us to consider the complexity of the concept of ethnicity as it relates to age and gender as well as the acculturation process. Developing a perspective that considers both sameness and difference, both within and between ethnic groups, is important because a focus on either without attention to the other will lead to distortion.

Diversity for Care Providers

Historically, responsibility for the ethnic client tended to be apportioned to the professional who shared the identifying characteristic, i.e., race. Congruity of provider/care recipient continues to be a strength in any delivery system. However, this match may be difficult, even when it appears congruent. African American health care providers know the variability of African American older persons. Language differences may make racial similarities an important but not sufficient basis for communication, as a example. Yet it is crucially important that the health care work force represent the ethnic diversity of the older population it serves. More than half the U.S. workforce now consists of minorities, immigrants and women (Thomas, 1990). It is important that diversity is represented within professions at all levels of status and authority (Antonucci & Cantor, 1994).

In Los Angeles 40% of the total population are non-Hispanic whites; this does not even account for the number of European immigrants. In this metropolis, the interface of ethnicity in service provision in long term care is often striking. At Keiro, a Japanese Nursing Home located in East Los Angeles, a Latino neighborhood, most of the residents are first generation Japanese and are monolingual Japanese, professionals are bilingual English and Japanese, and most of the aides are predominantly Spanish speaking Mexican

American and El Salvadorian immigrants. A related issue is the beliefs of elders that limit their access to multicultural assistance. Prejudice based on a life lived disproportionately in the acceptance of segregation may limit some persons' acceptance of diversity in late life leading them to not accept a provider of another racial or ethnic group.

Kavanaugh and Kennedy (1992) challenge professionals to affirm diversity not be proud to ignore it and state that "everyone is alike." Through reflective practice care providers must assess their shortcomings and stereotypes that limit their ability to appreciate difference. This can lead to a fuller appreciation of the variety of individual elders we have the opportunity to care for. Though diversity can beget conflict its acknowledgment can also promote and confirm difference in ways that may avert noncompliance to our care plans and interventions.

BI-CULTURAL AGING

The "one and only adventure in history" (Erikson, 1963) may have taken the older person across continents to build their life. Many ethnic elders have a life style created both from their country of origin or their families' country of origin and their country of residence. Confounding the elder's experience of ethnic identification in the U.S. is this biculturization or the different degrees to which the person is socialized in two cultures, contemporary American culture and the elder's culture of origin (Parrillo, 1996). This acculturation process produces the dual identity symbolized by the nomenclature of Chinese American or Hispanic American. Certainly a major dynamic in understanding ethnic differences is the variation among elders in the degree of acculturation and ethnic identification (Kitano, 1985). Ethnic identification of older adults must be viewed within this changing and sometimes conflicting context (Gelfand, 1994).

Even if the elder remained in the country of origin, industrialization, urbanization and modernization would take place and alter traditional cultural believes and create differences between generations and an emerging ethnic shift (Gelfand, 1994). Frequently cultural descriptions are taken unchanged from the country of origin and applied to the ethnic experience of an elder in this country.

Many have been influenced profoundly by sociopolitical and historical events in this country and abroad. Isei and Nisei or first and second generation Japanese American elders' dignity as well as economic status were shattered with the bombing of Pearl Harbor and the subsequent move to internment camps (Kitano, 1985). Immigrants of choice must be distinguished from those fleeing their country in need of political asylum. Cambodian elders immigrated to the U.S. fleeing war and torture (Lew, 1991). Refugees may have little social support, have left with out cherished belongings, and be psychologically bereft.

The strength of ethnic identification varies over the life course for any individual, by social context and within the historical context. For persons born at the turn of the century, assimilation based on a "melting pot" ideology was a cherished virtue (Healey, 1995). Not until the 1960s did ethnic pride emerge as an attribute of social value. Older persons as a cohort may have a much different view of the place of ethnicity in American culture than the baby boom generation. As older persons live outside of their traditional environments the saliency of ethnicity to their lives may weaken (Gelfand and Barresi, 1987). As an example, in a study of Japanese older adults they were found to use a combination of traditional and professional treatments reserving the later for more severe symptoms (Sakauye, 1990). The following examples of rituals and family care present additional ways in which bicultural influences apply to the care of ethnic elders.

Emerging Rituals in Providing Care

Rituals provide resources for ethnic identification and social exchange. Rituals are not immutable but can present the same fundamental symbolic meanings in a variety of forms tailored to suit various social circumstances. People old and young reshape aspects of their culture based in new environments (Gelfand, 1994). The rituals described here are in transition much as the individual's ethnic identification is modified not only by interaction with the majority culture but also by even broader contemporary dynamics.

Chin (1991) reveals changes in the hwangap or 70th birthday ritual for Korean elders that relate to industrialization and urbanization in Korea as well as to migration to the US and community formation in this country. Doi (1991) describes Japanese American kanreki or 60th birthday rituals which have changed between generations. In both these cases the birthday party which is distinctly western is substituted for aspects of the traditional celebration. The use of ritual to create community and late life integrity should be examined by service providers.

The blanket use of contemporary American traditions for all elders, many of which are organized as child's play, may lead to alienation rather than community. Social activities in senior centers and residential facilities which center around Halloween or St. Patrick's Day may totally lack meaning for the ethnic elder. A life without meaningful cultural ritual and ceremony, substituted with Valentine parties or Bingo, may add a sense of despair rather than integrity (Damron-Rodriguez, 1991). Doi's (1991) description of the making of a thousand cranes in celebration of old age for Japanese elders is an example of a culturally meaningful activity. In multiethnic facilities cultural exchanges between elders might facilitate communication between individuals and groups.

Emerging Family Care Issues

The family is a primary context for older persons care and is frequently viewed as particularly important for ethnic elders (Kahn & Antonnuci, 1980; Lubben & Becerra, 1987). Ethnic elders may be less likely to perceive themselves as frail within the context of culturally supported family care. Cambodians have expectations about independence that are markedly different from mainstream American views which form the basis for policy and program development in the U.S. (Lew, 1991). Southeast Asian elders value interdependence above independence. To be valued and respected is to be cared for by family. Thus, for these elders, promoting program participation on the basis of "maximizing independence" and avoiding being cared for by others would *not* increase participation.

A significant difference between minority and majority elder care is the number of older persons cared for in the home of children or younger family members (Hooyman & Kiyak, 1996). Unmarried older African-Americans are twice as likely to live with family as whites. Asians and Latinos are three times more likely than Anglos, even after controlling for income, health status, and other characteristics (Worobey & Angel, 1990).

There is reason to believe that this intergenerational living is a benefit and a challenge to family members (Brubaker, 1990; Cantor, 1994). In some cases for low income families the older person in the home may be an economic benefit as well as providing instrumental assistance (Worobey & Angel, 1990). The multiple responsibilities of minority families may also create significant costs in health and opportunity for the caregiver (Antonucci & Cantor, 1994). A distinction must be made between values and beliefs related to filial piety and what is actually realistic for families with multiple economic and role responsibilities in post-industrial society (Strawbridge & Wallhagen, 1992). Community based services will need to integrate with the informal network including not only family but friends, neighbors, churches and temples and other community services (Antonucci & Cantor, 1994). The family may need to be the "unit of care" not assuming that no community support is needed for immigrant families because "they take care of their own."

MINORITY ELDERLY

The "good and the bad" of ethnic elders' lives may be associated with, among other aspects of living, the positives and negatives of status in their adopted country. Minority status differs markedly from ethnicity. Ethnicity is predominantly self identification in contrast to minority status which is a comparison of differential power relationships between groups (Healey, 1995). Minority status limits access to a society's resources. Some ethnic groups, though few in relative number, do not experience minority status. Many ethnic elders experience poorer income and health in late life based on a lifetime of marginalized economic and social opportunities (Markides, Liang, & Jackson, 1990). Multicultural perspectives may appear to view ethnicity as an area of difference among equals (Parrillo, 1996). However, minority status is not to be overlooked because of its hard outcomes in differential morbidity and mortality throughout the life cycle (Wykle & Kaskel, 1994). Yet ethnicity in and of itself should not be conceived as a liability (Gelfand, 1994).

Thus, it is imperative to consider both the beliefs and values of ethnic elders which may furnish adaptive resources for challenges presented by minority status and aging itself (Stoller & Gibson, 1997). It is also important to view the integrity of a minority elders' lives within the context of a social structure of disadvantage and privilege. For African American elders their childhood was lived within a racially segregated world which presented a struggle to maintain self respect. Some adaptive resources to combat disadvantage are strong filial and religious ties. Yet many survivors of this hostile world over the life course often show in late life a remarkable resilience and strength (Antonucci & Cantor, 1994). This extraordinary survivorship has been related to the morbidity crossover for older African Americans who are often healthier in late life than would be projected (Markides, Liang, & Jackson, 1990).

Hooyman and Kiyak (1988) integrate these two contrasting dimensions of ethnic aging:

> Based on its unique history, each ethnic minority population developed its own methods of coping with the inevitable conflicts between traditional and adopted ways of life, leading to both vulnerabilities and strengths in the ways they adjust to aging. (p. 475)

Poverty

Minority elders in late life must attend to age discrimination and frailty along with minority status and thus, face what has been termed double jeopardy (Tally & Kaplan, 1956; Bengston, 1979). Even further triple jeopardy has been associated with older minority women who are confronted with a life course of gender as well as race discrimination (Dressel, 1988). Though double and triple jeopardy have been questioned as an over arching framework to view ethnic aging (Kiyak & Hooyman, 1996), minority older persons have significantly higher rates of poverty. In 1987, 10% of elderly whites, 34% of elderly African Americans, and 27 percent of elderly Hispanics were poor (AARP, 1989). Poverty is highest for older women in all groups (Quinn & Smeeding, 1994). Older African American men and women are the most likely to live in poverty. Of older African American women who live alone half live in poverty (Quinn & Smeeding, 1994).

Service Accessibility and Acceptability

Although minority older adults have higher service needs based on medical problems and functional limitations, they have lower utilization of key geriatric services (Damron-Rodriguez, Wallace, & Kington, 1994). Professionals must deliberately address two elements of the delivery system in order to provide equitable services for minority populations. The metaphor of the service door will be used to illustrate these elements. Accessibility requires opening the door to services for older adults while acceptability means that ethnic elders want to walk through the door (Damron-Rodriguez, Wallace, & Kington, 1994). Many service doors have signs that say welcome but to a place that is culturally closed. Opening the door requires that services are located in the community where the elders live, that admission procedures do not exclude elders based on immigration status and that language barriers do not bar admission.

Accessibility is created by addressing structural barriers including income, health care coverage, location of service, and transportation including accessibility for functional limitations including cognitive limitations. Kramer (1991) describes American Indian elders' abhorrence of the "white" tape that surrounds services and elders' unwillingness to accept services delivered as charity.

To create acceptable services, cultural barriers must be addressed. These include ethnic factors such as language, religion, family and acculturation. Some provider interventions include: outreach, translation, interpretation, transportation, cultural training for health professionals, and the use of bilingual/bicultural para-professionals. To maximize the quality and the equity of services to ethnic minority elderly, providers must accommodate racial and ethnic diversity while standardizing the provision of health services to assure equity in the types of services and interventions available to all older persons (Damron-Rodriguez, Wallace & Kington, 1992).

CONCLUSION

Modernization theory (Cowgill & Holmes, 1972) reminds us that urbanization, medicalization, and secularization are major social forces which reduce the worth of older persons. This challenge to the value of the aged is particularly salient to ethnic elders as they age in contemporary society. How then can care providers respect the dignity of ethnic elders who bring hard won strengths and frailties to late life and are tremendously diverse?

Barker (1994) provides a metaphor to help understand the cultural differences between care providers and ethnic elders. The "shooting star" describing the life trajectory of the professions will be compared with the "roller coaster" orientation of many ethnic elders.

> The *shooting star* has a straight path trajectory to the top always aiming to reach the best in life or the highest achievement. The steeper, straighter the trajectory the better. Life's path might be hard work and not much fun but the endpoint of unlimited resources and freedom are what counts. Time is of the essence and becomes a commodity that must be spent. Rationality, efficiency, and economy are prized. Keep your eye on the goal.
>
> Contrast that to the *roller coaster* model which sees life events as a series of ups and downs. These are endured and experienced and lived through. Where one is heading is constantly changing. There is no glorious destination. There are good times and bad times and nothing is forever. One person is not in control. One needs to be mobile and adjustable to contingencies. A person's life is best when part of a group. When one's own luck is out, someone else will be there. Pooling resources makes the ride smoother for all. Go with the flow, enjoy the ride. (Paraphrased, Barker, 1994, 15-17)

These different life views have consequences in their approach to providing care in late life. The medical model is based in doing "to" or "for" patients rather than "with" and as such may mitigate against respect. The approach of individual treatment planning and goal setting in order to maximize independence is a model for success to most care providers. The wait and see, more accepting approach of many elders may be viewed as resistance or noncompliance by the professional who proposes his goals to the elder and meets with less than enthusiasm. Leaving the family out of the plan as a short cut to intervention may lead to ultimate failure in the long run. These differences must be negotiated; both views may be valuable and contribute to positive care (Berlin & Fowkes, 1983).

The American health care system has traditionally acknowledged and emphasized individuals as the locus of problems and interventions (Kavanugh & Kennedy, 1992). Organizational and disciplinary culture focus on individuals as the "units of service." In the changing health care environment health care providers are asked to change perspective, if not paradigm, to view the individual within the context of their community (Grant & Finnocchio, 1995).

The dynamics of dignity and respect appreciate that care provision is an interpersonal/interactive process. It requires the care provider to be reflective and appreciate the way in which their own beliefs and values influence the care. Increasingly, in late life a person's worth is mirrored by professionals who know little about the individual as a person rather than a patient. Further, to understand the individual the richness of a long life must be brought to the foreshortened life perspective of the very old. Communication and meaning in the delivery of care is an important interactional process in respecting the tremendous ethnic and cultural diversity of those served. It requires the skill of inquiry, asking others for their view of the care they receive and its meaning. This can be done in groups when we seek direction for our programs and individually in our practice. We must be watchful for constrictions in our services which require elders to adapt and conform to a limited set of norms in order to access resources.

Wu (1975) described the process of adjustment to life in Los Angeles for Chinese elders as the "adaptable art of living" that was required to grow old gracefully in a foreign country. This is exemplified in the Chinese proverb "Youth is a gift of nature; Age is a work of art." A similar artful adaptation is required of service providers in order to adapt care that is both accessible and acceptable for ethnic elders. Care providers may give valuable materials or resources for this "work of art." However, they do not supply the canvas or the background for the elder's life. The canvas is the life course or history of each ethnic elder. The form and texture of the work is envisioned through the cultural lens of the elder. The artist is the elder who alone, but with support, can create the life of integrity and dignity. It is the care provider's work to appreciate the contribution and preserve the creation. That is respectful care. In the end, any contribution to the dignity of our elders will be an intergenerational one. For as Erikson (1963) proposes, "children will not fear life if their elders have the integrity not to fear death."

Epilogue or Something

> But in the main, I feel like a brown bag of miscellany propped against a wall. Against a wall in company with other bags, white, red and yellow. Pour out the contents, and there is discovered a jumble of small things priceless and worthless, a first water diamond, an empty spool, bits of broken glass, lengths of string, a key to a door long since crumbled away, a rusty knife-blade, old shoes saved for a road that never was and never will be, a nail bent under the weight of things too heavy for any nail, a dried flower or two still a little fragrant. In your hand is the brown bag. On the ground before you is the jumble it held so much like the jumble in the other bags, it could be emptied and all might be dumped into a single heap. Perhaps that is the way the Great Stuffer of Bags filled them in the first place–who knows?

> –Zora Neale Hurston, *How it Feels to be Colored Me* (c. 1922)

Nowhere to put this but couldn't quite get rid of it yet. Says something to our uniformity as well as our diversity–wanted to share it!

REFERENCES

ARRP Minority Affairs Initiative (1988). *A portrait of older minorities*. Washington, DC: American Association of Retired Persons.

Antonucci, T.C. & Cantor, M.H. (1994). Strengthening the family support system for older minority persons. In *Minority elders: Longevity, economics, and health* (2nd Ed.). Gerontological Society of America, p. 40.

Barker, J.C. (1994). Recognizing cultural differences: Health-care providers and elderly patients. *Cultural Diversity and Geriatric Care: Challenges to the Health Professions*. New York: The Haworth Press, Inc.

Barresi, C.M. (1987). Ethnic Aging and the Life Course. pp. 18-34.

Bateson, M.C. (1990). *Composing a Life*. New York: Plume.

Bengston, V.L. (1979). Ethnicity and aging: Problems and issues in current social science inquiry. In D.E. Gelfand and A.J. Kutzik (Eds.), *Ethnicity and aging: Theory, research and policy.* New York: Springer, 9-31.

Berlin, E.A., & Fowkes, W.C. (1983). A teaching framework for cross-cultural health care. *The Western Journal of Medicine, 139,* 934-938.

Brubaker, T.N. (1990). Families in later life: A burgeoning research area. *Journal of Marriage and the Family, 52,* 959-981.

Cantor, M. (1994). Family caregiving: Social care. In M. Cantor (Ed.), *Family caregiving: Agenda for the future.* San Francisco, CA: American Society on Aging, 1-9.

Chatters, L.M., & Taylor, R.J. (1994). Religious involvement among older African-Americans. In J.S. Levin (Ed.) *Religion in aging and health: Theoretical foundations and methodological frontiers.* Thousand Oaks, CA: Sage, pp. 196-230.

Chau, P., Lee, H., Tseng, R., & Downers, N.J. (1990). Dietary habits, health beliefs, and food practices of elderly Chinese women. *Journal of the American Dietetic Association, 90*(4), 579-580.

Chin, S.Y. (1991). Korean birthday rituals. *Journal of Cross-Cultural Gerontology, 6*(2), 145.

Cowgill, D. & Holmes, L. (1972). *Aging and Modernization.* New York: Appleton-Century-Crofts.

Cox, C. (1993). The Frail Elderly: Problems, Needs, and Community Responses. *Ethnicity and Frailty.* Westport, CN: Auburn House, pp. 125-145.

Damron-Rodriguez, J.A. (1991). Multicultural aspects of aging in the U.S.: Implications for health and human services. *Journal of Cross-Cultural Gerontology, 6*(2), 135-145.

Damron-Rodriguez, J.A., Wallace, S., & Kington, R. (1994). Service utilization and minority elderly: Appropriateness, accessibility, and acceptability. *Cultural diversity and geriatric care. Challenges to the Health Professions.* New York: The Haworth Press, Inc.

Dressel, P. (1988). Gender, race and class: Beyond the feminization of poverty in later life. *The Gerontologist, 28*(2), 177-180.

Erikson, E. (1963). *Childhood and society.* New York: Norton.

Frank, J., Damron-Rodriguez, J.A., Levin, J., Hirsch, S., & Reuben, D.B. (1995). Multicultural perceptions of the meaning of health. A presentation at the 48th Annual Scientific Meeting of the Scientific Meeting of the Gerontology Society of America, Los Angeles, CA.

Frank, J, Damron-Rodriguez, J.A., Hirsch, S., & Reuben, D. (1995). A paper presentation at the 50th Annual Scientific Meeting of the Gerontology Society of America in Los Angeles, CA.

Gelfand, D.E. (1994). *Aging and ethnicity: Knowledge and services.* New York: Springer Publishing Company.

Gelfand, D.E. & Yee, B. (1992). Trends and forces: Influence of immigration, migration, and acculturation on the fabric of aging in America. *Generations, 15*(4), 7-10.

Grant, R.W. & Finocchio, L.J. (1995). The California Primary Care Consortium on Interdisciplinary Collaboration: A Model Curriculum and Resource Guide. San Francisco, CA: Pew Health Professions Commission.

Holzberg, C. (1982). Ethnicity and aging: Anthropological perspectives on more than just the minority elderly. *The Gerontologist, 22,* 249-257.

Hooyman, N. & Kiyak, H.A. (1988). *Social gerontology.* Boston: Allyn & Bacon.

Kaufman, S.R. (1986). *The Ageless Self: Sources of Meaning in Late Life.* Wisconsin: University of Wisconsin Press.

Kavanagh, K.H. & Kennedy, P.H. (1992). *Promoting Cultural Diversity: Strategies for Health Care Professionals.* Newbury Park, CA: Sage Publications.

Kramer, B.J. (1991). Urban American Indian aging. *Journal of Cross-Cultural Gerontology, 6*(2), 205.

Kahn, R.L. & Antonucci, T.C. (1980). Convoys over the life course: Attachment, roles, and social support. In P.B. Baltes & O.G. Brim (Eds.), *Life span development and behavior* (Vol. 3, pp. 253-286). New York: Academic Press.

Levin, J.S., Markides, K.S. & Ray, L. (1996). Religious attendance and psychological well-being in Mexican Americans: A panel study analysis of three-generations data. *The Gerontologist, 36*(4), 455-463.

Levin, J.S & Tobin, S.S. (1995). Religion and psychological well-being. In M.S. Kimble, S.H. McFadden, J.W. Ellor & J.J. Seeber (Eds.), *Aging, spirituality, and religion: A handbook.* Minneapolis: Fortress Press, pp. 30-46.

Lew, L.S. (1991). Elderly Cambodians in Long Beach: Creating cultural access to health care. *Journal of Cross-Cultural Gerontology, 6*(2), 199.

Litwak, E. (1985). *Helping the elderly.* New York: The Guilford Press.

Lustbader, W. (1991). *Counting on kindness.* New York: Free Press.

Markides, K., Liang, J., & Jackson, J. (1990). Race, ethnicity and aging. In R. Binstock, R. & George, L. (Eds.), *Handbook of aging and the social sciences: Third edition.* San Diego, CA: Academic Press.

Neufeldt, V. & Guralnik, D.B. (1991). *Webster's New World Dictionary.* New York: Simon & Schuster.

Osako, M.M. (1979). Aging and family among Japanese Americans: The role of ethnic tradition in the adjustment to old age. *The Gerontologist, 19*(5), 448-455.

Quinn, J.F. & Smeeding, T.M. (1994). Defying the averages: Poverty and well-being among older Americans. *Aging Today,* September/October, XV(5), 9.

Sakauye, K. (1990). Differential diagnosis, medication, treatment, and outcomes: Asian American elderly. In *Minority aging.* Rockville, MD: U.S. Department of Health and Human Services.

Stoller, E.P. & Gibson, R.C. (1997). *Worlds of Difference: Inequality in the Aging Experience.* Thousand Oaks, CA: Pine Forge Press.

Tally, T. & Kaplan, J. (1956). The Negro aged. *Gerontological Society Newsletter, 3.*

Thomas, R.R. (1990). From Affirmative Action to affirming diversity. *Harvard Business Review,* March-April, pp. 107-117.

Valle, R. (1989). U.S. ethnic minority group access to long-term care. In *Caring for an aging world: International models for long-term care, financing and delivery.* New York: McGraw-Hill Information Services Company.

Worobey, J.L., & Angel, R.I. (1990). Poverty and health: Older minority women and the rise of the female-headed household. *Journal of Health and Social Behavior, 31*(4), 370-383.

Wykle, M. & Kaskel, B. (1994). Increasing the longevity of minority older adults through improved health status. In *Minority elders: Longevity, economics, and health* (2nd Ed.). Gerontological Society of America, p. 32.

Spirituality and Community
in the Last Stage of Life

Henry C. Simmons, PhD

The title of this paper, "Spirituality and Community in the Last Stage of Life," puts together three concepts which belong together. This essay will show the necessary interrelationship of spirituality, community, and the last stage of life, and will draw out some implications of this interrelationship for "aging with dignity."

I begin with a conviction: the last years of life cannot be adequately described without attention to a struggle to keep the human spirit from being overwhelmed by frailty. I describe this as a spiritual struggle. As Maurice Sendak was quoted as saying, "There must be more to life than having everything." Indeed there is. And at a time of life when "having everything" is less and less an option, it is critical to search out and affirm that "something more to life."

INITIAL RESEARCH:
THOSE WHO WORK WITH THE FRAIL OLD

My conviction that the last years of life are adequately described only when we admit their essentially spiritual nature led me to assume that people who work with the oldest old and treat them with dignity do so, at least in part, because they recognize their spiritual struggles and are willing to share in them. I began speaking

---

[Haworth co-indexing entry note]: "Spirituality and Community in the Last Stage of Life." Simmons, Henry C. Co-published simultaneously in *Journal of Gerontological Social Work* (The Haworth Press, Inc.) Vol. 29, No. 2/3, 1998, pp. 73-91; and: *Dignity and Old Age* (ed: Robert Disch, Rose Dobrof, and Harry R. Moody) The Haworth Press, Inc., 1998, pp. 73-91. Single or multiple copies of this article are available for a fee from The Haworth Document Delivery Service [1-800-342-9678, 9:00 a.m. - 5:00 p.m. (EST). E-mail address: getinfo@haworthpressinc.com].

73

with this group because they were a fair cross-section of the reader-
ship of this book.

Thus I interviewed some people who work with the frail old,
asking about their sense of motivation for treating the old with
dignity. Although my sample was small and unscientific, I found
two common threads: (1) they treat the old with dignity because
they treat everyone with dignity; and (2) they treat everyone with
dignity because of something that happened to them years ago.

One woman told this story:

> I grew up in a small town. When my parents divorced in the
> early 60's people disapproved. We were poor, then, too. I
> always wore second-hand clothes. I got taunted for that.
> Church didn't help. We got 'fire and brimstone' preaching. I
> knew what it was like to be the underdog. When I was 21, I
> went to a church where I found comfort and a sense of accep-
> tance. I heard the words, 'By grace you have been saved.' For
> the first time I felt I didn't have to earn grace, love, respect–in
> that church these were givens. It totally changed my life.

Later she added, "I'd like to think I don't treat the old with any
more dignity than I treat anyone else."

Another woman spoke of her love for relatives who lived nearby
as she grew up. Their sense of compassion stood in stark contrast
with her parents' judgmental views, so my friend chose to spend
time with these aunts and uncles. They lived up to a favorite saying,
"There's so much good in the worst of us, so much bad in the best
of us, that it behooves none of us to demean the rest of us." She
gave an example of an incident that had marked her as a child. A
neighbor wanted to put an addition on his garage so he could repair
cars from his home. Her uncle's response was, "So what if our
property values go down a bit; this is his livelihood."

These two women are not singular. Many I interviewed had
similar stories. With some variation, they learned young to treat
everyone in a certain way, and this was tied to personal experience
in households of conviction or communities of faith.

As I spoke with this group it became clear that the dignity they
afforded those in the last stage of life does not depend on any
special quality intrinsic to the old. In the precise language of the

Oxford English Dictionary (2nd edition), the way in which they related to people is better described as "dignifying" than "treating with dignity." To dignify is "to make worthy or illustrious, to confer dignity or honour upon, to invest with dignity or honour" (OED, 1989, p. 656). This is not the same as treating the old with dignity because they are "worthy, honourable, excellent (in nature, station, or estimation)" (*ibidem*). In the first case, dignity and honor are conferred; in the second the person is intrinsically worthy, honorable, or excellent.

Others whom I interviewed answered differently. For them, those in the last stage of life were at a time of life and dealing with issues that were of such weight that they approached those in the last stage of life with great diffidence. A woman who works with the frailest old reflected, "This is an intense place–the sense of the immediacy of the end of life makes it that. I love these people. But sometimes I feel threatened." I hear in these words echoes of Otto's description of the holy as *tremendum et fascinans*. One is attracted ("I love these people") but one does not enter their space lightly ("Sometimes I feel threatened.") It is the immediacy of the end of life that charges the moral atmosphere. The "now" becomes critical because it exists at the end of the life cycle.

In these people the emphasis had shifted. Those in the last stage of life had an intrinsic quality of dignity that evoked a certain response. This perspective is the one taken in this chapter. I retain the first perspective for two reasons: it was quite common, and it is grounded in communities of faith or households of conviction. The latter point will be critical in the development of this chapter.

THE LAST YEARS: TESTING THE HUMAN SPIRIT

The last years of life cannot be adequately described in meager concepts. It is a time of struggle as human frailty threatens to overcome the quality of this lived life, to overwhelm the human spirit. This frailty can be physical: for most in old age there is a time when sight, hearing, taste, smell grow dim or dark. The frailty can be mental: some are cast into the darkness of social isolation, relegated to live with the old or as the old, under the shadow of a collective cultural judgment that oldness is of no worth. For some, there is a lessening of mental powers: words are lost, wit becomes less quick, judgment becomes impaired. Frailty can be of the spirit: some report profound feelings of dislocation, anger, uselessness, loneliness.

The last stage of life is a time of endings: a time when one must often deal with suffering, with aloneness, almost certainly with dependency–perhaps with dignity and perhaps not–and finally with death. These are substantial realities; they touch every dimension of the person; they are realities most of us would prefer not to face at any age. In the end, though, there is little choice. A woman writes from her nursing home, "This is my world now. It's all I have left. You see, I'm old. And, I'm not as healthy as I used to be. I'm not necessarily happy with it but I accept it" (Seagrim, 1994, p. 11). This is not a struggle that one chooses; neither is it a struggle that many can avoid. In the last few decades medical care has moved to the point where death by degenerative disease is our likely fate. "This then is their quandary," says Robert Blythe, "slow motion departure" (1979, p. 73).

It might be argued that to speak of the last stage of life as a spiritual journey is to romanticize these years. Nevertheless this metaphor has power. Negatively, it gives a basis for challenge to self-indulgence, for criticism of what Blythe calls an unchecked "indulgent stupidity" (1979, p. 22) that can be part of the last years. It is of the nature of spiritual journeys or struggles that they can end in failure. Positively, it catches a sense of heroic and risk-filled tasks undertaken with others–marks of successful aging, where the journey is to death and the stake is the human spirit. It also leaves room for aggressiveness, independence, individualism, interdependence, competitiveness, future orientation and the like–qualities seldom praised as virtues in older adults.

A question might be raised about whether or not, in stressing the essentially spiritual nature of their struggle, we are holding those who are old to a higher standard than the standard we set for ourselves. The question is legitimate. To assign the notion of spiritual journey in a particular way to one part of the life cycle may abet the marginalization of the old. One could argue however in a somewhat different vein. In making demands of those who are in the last stage of life, we are setting ourselves up for those demands to be made of ourselves when we are old. The old are separated from us only by time. We are the not-yet-old. But in making demands of others we also implicate and enmesh ourselves in a community of discourse and meaning that prizes the spiritual journey. We are thus in a very real sense putting demands on ourselves.

It is possible to deny the spiritual nature of the last stage of life for a variety of reasons, some of which have to do with the profound secularization of the life-cycle and of death that is a hallmark of our culture. It is also possible that the burdens of the last stage of life are so unattractive that death seems preferable. The less courageous, those more like us perhaps, may obliquely affirm the essentially spiritual nature of the struggle in their explicit reluctance to engage themselves. The 15th century Dialogues of Catherine of Genoa end with a witty comment on the human capacity to avoid real issues at the end of life. *Spirit*, that noble and transcendent part of the human person, says to that part of the same person called *Human Frailty*, "You will live among the sick in great humility as long as I see fit and do so without interruption. I intend to go on living in this fashion, pure and clean as the moment of my creation. I will go to any lengths to assure that." *Human Frailty* answers, "Taking into account your resolve, my answer will be brief. I put myself in your hands and hope for a speedy death" (Hughes, 1979, pp. 129-130).

SPIRITUALITY

Spirituality is the quality of a lived life, seen from the inside. Spirituality refers to *embodied* realities that have to do with beauty, goodness, and truth—realities that touch the depth of the human person rather than simply stay on the surface of the person. The word "spirituality" is not the opposite of "bodiliness." Indeed, it is through the fragile language of the body that we apprehend the mystery of the world, of others, of the Other. Spirituality does not deny bodily flesh. But neither does it admit the adequacy of any technical language of the body (e.g., physics, cell biology, medicine) to describe human persons.

The language of spirituality as it concerns the last stage of life may arise in a community that describes itself as religious; it may equally arise in a community of discourse that does not appeal to religious language. In non-religious language, spirituality can be fleshed out (pun intended) along these lines. Life is described as spiritual as it refers to the intensity of the whole person, to qualities of humanness, presence, depth. It is the opposite of bodiliness only to the extent that bodiliness refers to the human person seen exclusively from the outside. When people bear responsibility, live as they would like to live, combat the temptation to inner despair, or keep chaos from invading the center–there is the stuff of spirituality.

In a *Newsweek* article, "My World Now: Life in a nursing home, from the inside," Anna Mae Halgrim Seaver reflects on her present life. Her language is not religious, yet her acceptance of her difficult life–an acceptance that resists despair–rises from the depths of a very noble human spirit:

> Most of us are aware of our plight–some are not. [. . .] I don't much like some of the physical things that happen to us. I don't care much for a diaper. I seem to have lost the control acquired so diligently as a child. The difference is that I'm aware and embarrassed but I can't do anything about it. (1994, p. 11)

She ends her reflections, "This is my world now. It's all I have left. You see, I'm old. And, I'm not as healthy as I used to be. I'm not necessarily happy with it but I accept it."

Within Judeo-Christian traditions, spirituality uses a language of grace, relationship of the human person to God, the human response to the indwelling Spirit. There are great religious themes that can be applied in particular ways in the last stage of life: repentance, reconciliation, reparation; resurrection, redemption; resting in the bosom of Abraham; the vision of God face to face. Religious language runs the risk of so spiritualizing the human condition that the essential bodiliness of human life is lost, but it need not do so. Julian of Norwich, a 14th century English mystic, writes:

> A man walks upright, and the food in his body is shut up as if in a well-made purse. When the time of his necessity comes, the purse is opened and then shut again, in most seemly fashion. And it is God who does this. [. . .] We are, soul and body,

clad and enclosed in the goodness of God. (*Julian of Norwich Showings*, p. 186)

Hard realities are also faced in a religious description of the spiritual journey. For example, John of the Cross describes what he calls the dark night of the spirit:

> God [. . .] leaves the intellect in darkness, the will in aridity, the memory in emptiness, and the affections in supreme affliction, bitterness, and anguish, by depriving the soul of the feeling and satisfaction it previously obtained from spiritual blessings. (Kavanaugh, 1987, p. 186)

In explicitly religious language the acceptance of profound darkness of spirit is linked to growth and depth. It is my conviction that both explicitly religious and not explicitly religious "language sets" point to the same truth. In the end, Anna Mae Halgrim Seaver and John of the Cross are sister and brother, as each embraces a reality that touches into the depth of the human person in this last stage of life.

COMMUNITY AND SPIRITUALITY

So far I have described some elements of spirituality in the last stage of life. The task in this section is to show the interrelationship of *community* with spirituality in the last stage of life. However, I acknowledge at least four reasons why one might rather connect spirituality with the *individual* in the last stage of life: we know admirable individuals who appear to have come to a deep sense of spirituality on their own; there is a literature of spirituality for the last stage of life that addresses the individual; there is no common sense that the life cycle is sacred; and, specifically, a formerly wide-spread Protestant vision of life as a spiritual voyage no longer prevails.

Spirituality as an Individual Pursuit

There are gifted individuals who appear to have come to a deep sense of spirituality on their own. Indeed, we could hardly speak about spirituality in the last stage of life if we did not have witnesses to the possibilities of that age. A video called *Water From Another Time* tells the story of three outstanding people. It ends with the reflection:

> In the vast space of the imagination, it is possible to hold the past in the present and youth in old age. The appeal to memory is a quest for meaning. Lois Doane, Lotus Dickey, and Elmer Boyd are experts at drawing up meaning from the well of memory. In their solitude they create an account of their experience.

In video and film, biography and autobiography, in people known personally or through others, we come in contact with heroic individuals who "in their solitude create an account of their experience." This is the first reason to consider the essentially individual nature of spirituality in old age: we find real instances of individuals who make sense for themselves of an otherwise chaotic world. Theirs are not universally-held stories. For all their power they are personal narratives that sustain a vision of the human in the last stage of life.

Secondly, there is a literature for spirituality in the last stage of life that specifically addresses the individual. I am not referring here to a predictably individualistic self-help, new age kind of writing. In Christian devotional literature addressed to the old the common concern is the specific contribution of religious faith to the realities of growing old, of being old, and of dying. With rare exceptions, these materials stress spirituality and right action as individual concerns. Their primary use is as texts of private devotion. Christian churches, at least, do not have many developed curricular materials for teaching about spirituality in the last stage of life (Simmons, 1995a). In large measure, these *communities* of faith do not see spirituality in the last stage of life as a *communal* concern.

Thirdly, there is no longer a common sense of the sacredness of the life-cycle. Historical and cultural analyses show the weakening of a collective sense of meaning. In a culture that does not value old age as having intrinsic worth, people are left on their own to try to find some meaning for *their* old age.

> Then in the twentieth century, the collective sense of meaning in turn has weakened, leaving us with an exclusively individual preoccupation with the meaning of life. [. . .] In other words, retreating to a private sphere of meaning is the best we can hope for in a disordered and meaningless world. [. . .] This retreat to privatism is an unsatisfactory solution to questions about the meaning of life and the meaning of old age. (Moody, 1986, p. 13)

Fourthly, a formerly wide-spread Protestant vision of life as a spiritual voyage no longer prevails. The Calvinist vision of life promoted by the Puritans had very specific meanings for the last stage of life: long life was a sign of God's predilection, and a "good" death was devoutly prayed for. This understanding of the last stage of life, once widespread, no longer holds.

> The demise of the old Protestant vision of life as a spiritual voyage meant that no one came forward any longer to defend old age on the grounds that old people had more important business to attend to—for example, meeting final obligations to God, family, community, and self. (Cole, 1986, p. 126)

Cumulatively, these four lines of approach seem to argue compellingly that we ought to speak of *individuality* and spirituality rather than *community* and spirituality in the last stage of life. Nevertheless, I remain convinced of the intrinsic connection between community and spirituality in the last stage of life. In spite of their cogency, the four points just presented do not deal a fatal blow to this conviction.

Gifted individuals who come to a profound sense of spirituality in the last stage of life are just that—gifted. Not everyone can develop this depth of spirituality apparently without the support of others. Further, some gifted individuals with whom I have spoken have pointed out to me the roots of their present insights in communal visions of the life course.

Some Christian devotional literature, like some secular literature, runs against a general individualistic thrust in the literature of spirituality in the last stage of life. Books like *Aging as Counterculture: A vocation for the later years* (Maitland, 1991) and *The Older We*

Get . . . An action guide to social change (Hoffman, 1985) stand alongside secular counterparts like *Altruism in Later Life* (Midlarsky & Kahana, 1994) and *Voices and Visions of Aging: Toward a critical gerontology* (Cole et al., 1993). These are instances of approaches that are more communal than individualistic. While such approaches are not mainstream they do represent a genuine option to an exclusively individualistic spirituality in late life.

The weakening of a collective sense of the sacredness of the life-cycle and the demise of the old Protestant vision of life do not necessarily imply the absence of all common meaning for old age. Dominant cultural metaphors of aging make quite clear sense–or more specifically non-sense–of the last stage of life. The old are portrayed negatively as the not-young, the not-physically strong, the not-productive–witness advertisements, birthday cards, the absence of representation of creative older adults in TV culture, and so on. While negative, this is still a meaning–or non-meaning–given to old age. It is, of course, clearly inimical to any public, positive sense of meaning and to the self understanding of the person in the last stage of life.

Spirituality and Community in the Last Stage of Life

While this negative "spirituality" may be appropriated by the individual, it may also be resisted and replaced. As I will argue in the section that follows, it is more likely that it be resisted and a new and adequate sense of a spirituality appropriate to the age be developed in an intentional community of discourse and support. Human world-building and meaning-making are collective enterprises. In the absence of universally-held stories that make sense of the last stage of life we must choose communities of discourse that support a spirituality that is adequate to the tasks of late old age.

It is not my intention to argue the case that meaning arises in community. I assume a consensus that human "world-building is always a collective enterprise," sustained by conversation with significant others. "The internal appropriation of a world must [. . .] take place in a collectivity" (Berger, 1967, p. 16). Although no positive corporate meaning can be found, there are individuals who come to a satisfactory and profoundly spiritual sense of their lives. This does not mean however that a sense of the rightness of the life course and its exigencies is only possible on an individual basis. Between a culture of negative meaning and the intensely personal meaning of gifted individuals stand intentional communities of meaning.

> The deconstruction of nature is part of a wider 'disenchant-ment of the world' (Weber). But it does not imply that narra-tives, grand or otherwise, are impossible; it only requires that we choose them consciously and in dialogue with one another. (Moody, 1995, p. 17)

INTENTIONAL COMMUNITIES OF DIALOGUE AND SUPPORT

I will describe some conditions under which a community fo-cused on the concerns of those in the last stage of life will success-fully affirm in substantial and sustaining ways what it is to age with dignity. First, though, it may be well to offer a couple of examples of what this might look like in real life. A Rabbi writes of her chaplaincy in a nursing home.

> In our nursing home, we live not just in 'institutional time' but in 'Jewish time.' [. . .]
> Living in Jewish time, we celebrate every Jewish holiday. We do not just celebrate Shabbat and other joyous, affirming days but also Tisha B'Av, a relatively obscure and somber fast day. When we complete the service for Tisha B'Av, with some 60 residents in attendance [. . .] Mrs. A. remarks, 'It was wonderful!' [. . .] What was 'wonderful' was that through this ritual, Mrs. A. and her fellow congregants had an opportunity to be taken seriously, to share a part of their experience, to cry and grieve together and to know that our tradition recognizes and affirms these feelings as well. Loss and suffering are a part of their life, and Judaism provides a time for acknowledging them. (Friedman, 1991, pp. 15-16)

In this example, the celebration of Tisha B'Av is a deliberately chosen narrative that is part of a religious tradition; in the example that follows the narrative is more local, but the embodied vision of aging with dignity is very real.

> Our community meetings were always open to all. Participants included those who were well and those who were suffering from the ravages of broken bones that failed to heal, arthritis, Alzheimer's and other dementias, Parkinson's, advanced cancer, and other diseases.
> We told the residents repeatedly that we saw (and we continue to see) ourselves as building a movement for change—right here in a nursing home at the bottom of society's pecking order. The underlying theme in our discussions was that no matter how disabled a person might be, there is still something healthy, alive, and vital within him or her that can grow and expand and promote healing in the self and in others. Our lifeline is in our connection to one another. (Barkan, 1995, pp. 174-175)

In a hospitable learning space obedience to the truth can be practiced (Palmer, 1983). In the communities of meaning described above, we see lived out "we believe" narratives that affirm in substantial and sustaining ways spiritualities that support aging with dignity. These communities have created hospitable spaces where obedience to the truth is practiced.

In the section that follows, I articulate in more linear fashion some of the characteristics of communities of dialogue where bonds are forged that allow for the growth of the human spirit in the last stage of life. No doubt one could propose many characteristics of communities of dialogue that support aging with dignity. In this section I identify three such characteristics that, if absent, would jeopardize a communal development of an adequate spirituality. No doubt there are others (for example, the willingness to grieve loss). The three I propose are (a) embracing a dream, (b) supporting a quest for meaning, and (c) encouraging a search for freedom.

Embracing a Dream

I have already given two examples of communities that support aging with dignity. In each case, but in varying degree, there was a sense that something was rejected and something was chosen. In the first case, it was a rejection of institutional time–*chronus*, time by the clock–that leaves institutionalized elders in a chronic state of waiting–for a meal, for a bath, to have a bed made, to see a TV show. In place of this was put Jewish time–a rhythm of times and seasons that supports people in joy, in grief, in making sense. In the second example what was rejected was a world described by others as being at the bottom of the pecking order, even in nursing home terms–the world of the most frail, the aphasic, those suffering with dementias. In its place was put a way of being that was regenerative–that assumed the possibility of growth, expansion, and healing of self and others.

Both dimensions must be present: a collective rejection of the way one is "named" and a collective embracing of a new order. I have argued elsewhere (Simmons 1988, 1990) that it is not enough to retreat into what is ultimately a "collective privatism"–a community that finds strength and meaning disengaged from the culture. If men and women live long enough they will, in all likelihood, find they no longer fit the picture of what mainstream society judges to be normatively and authentically human–namely to be productive, to look young, to be physically well and strong. Unless cultural metaphors of aging are confronted they may ultimately erode the spirit.

Engaged communities recognize that they stand under the oppression of cultural metaphors and images. This is critical if a group is to move from the experience of the *problems* of aging to a dawning sense of agency for individuals and for the group. Genuine dialogue that does not resist the cliches of the culture is the starting point for a recognition that the culture's judgments on old age are not for the sake of those who are experiencing the last stage of life. It is only in this recognition that the possibility of a social order geared to authentic human need can be seen. It is only in this recognition that prophetic images able to support an adequate spirituality can become rich and profuse. Freedom is experienced dialectically, first in

the intention of rejecting the absolute ultimacy of the formerly dominant regime and, second, in the sense that by our own agency we can create a new history which is moving away from the oppressive forms of the present. (Sullivan, 1984, p. 95)

There is no expectation of a quick or dramatic cultural shift. There is, however, a group fearlessness, toughness, and creativity that takes as a starting-point for its own dialogue a recognition and refusal of the norms of a cultural context.

Supporting a Quest for Meaning

The second characteristic of a community committed to aging with dignity is that it support individual quests for meaning. In many ways this point is connected with the previous one. The difference is the focus in this section on the individual's need to work out his or her sense of truth, of making sense, of answering life "Whys?" In the context of larger narratives about human existence in the last stage of life, individuals create personal meaning in ways that differ widely. Midlarsky and Kahana (1995) list some of these ways: like Tolstoy, in a simple life and in faith in God; like Mishima, the Japanese novelist, in beauty; like Frankl, in each person's interpretation of life.

Personal interpretations may be as diverse as seeking meaning in contentment from gratification and from one's achievement; enjoying the pleasure of well-earned rest; searching for peak experiences in religious or humanistic exploration; through employment, philanthropy, creative pursuits, or in a dedication to the welfare of others. This dedication is particularly sustaining of spirituality in the last stage of life.

> Also inherent in the recognition of the significance of other lives is the recognition that one's own life and life in general are significant. Particularly for older adults, for whom mortality is imminent, humanitarian concerns may, therefore, reflect a commitment to life itself. (Midlarsky and Kahana, 1995, p. 225)

Meaning is a common human quest for a map, known or felt, that guides decisions and action, that gives coherence to life, that weaves past, present and future together in continuity, that shapes patterns of behavior in relation to the common and uncommon challenges of life (Rolland, 1994). To seek for meaning is then to ask in some way what is at stake in my life. It is here that we see the connection of aging, spirituality, and community in the last stage of life. To be in the last stage of life is, by definition, to be near the end of one's life. To the extent that one can deal with the fact that there is little time left, finding a personal rightness about life is an increasingly urgent task. Moore reflects,

> Growing old is one of the ways the *soul* nudges itself into attention to the spiritual aspect of life. The body's changes teach us about fate, time, nature, mortality, and character. Aging forces us to decide what is important in life." (1992, p. 216)

"Deciding what is important in my life" and "figuring out what is a stake in my life" are two ways of speaking about the centrality of meaning in human life. These very personal quests of the human spirit will be have a better chance of success in communities of dialogue that sustain the quest in substantial and supportive ways.

We may see this with special clarity in its absence.

> It is difficult to hold to one's own sense of self, to one's own dignity when all around you there is no affirmation of you. At best there may be a patronizing acknowledgement; at worst, you simply do not exist.
>
> The oppressed old woman is required to be cheerful. But if you are smiling all the time, you acquiesce to being invisible and docile, participating in your own "erasure." (Healey, 1986, in Stoller, Gibson, 1994, p. 83)

"Erasure" is such a powerful image for the threat of non-meaning possible when "there is no affirmation of you." This speaks eloquently of the need for a community that supports and sustains spirituality in the last stage of life.

Encouraging a Search for Freedom

To be free can mean to be oneself, to be unfettered, to speak forthrightly with one's own voice, to tell the truth, to forgive oneself

and others, to blame and accuse, to uncover family myths, to un-
mask social ills, to claim one's own fragile truth. All these facets of
freedom are, in varying degrees, part of the substance and content
of the last stage of life.

The urge to be free is lifelong. For example, just a few days
before her death, the principal character in Margaret Laurence's *The
Stone Angel* reflects on the lie she has just told her second son–that
he was always a better son to her than his now-dead brother.

> I lie here and try to recall something truly free that I have done
> in ninety years. I can think of only two acts that might be so,
> both recent. One was [. . .] a lie–yet not a lie, for it was spoken
> at least and at last with what may perhaps be a kind of love.
> (Laurence, 1964, p. 307)

Issues of freedom are not unique to older adults–generally speaking adults of all ages feel they are thinking and acting freely. But for
most the parameters of freedom in the earlier adult years are quite
narrow, regardless of whether we look at the personal/familial
world, the world of peers, or the wider political world. In the per-
sonal/familial world freedom is constrained by commitments, by
personal history, by the dynamics of the unconscious, and by larger
economic and social forces. In the world of peers, freedom is
constrained by trend and fashion, by the need to please, by the
tyranny of paycheck and bills, by circles of friends who expect and
reinforce group values. In the wider political world freedom is
constrained by fear and social unrest, by the isolation of far suburbs,
by media reinforcement of sound-bite thinking, by political processes that seems to offer few real choices.

Some of these constraints lessen with age. Thus, freedom may be
more possible in the later years than in the younger years. This is
not to romanticize old age. One can be as constrained, as unreflec-
tive, and as unfree at 89 as at 39. No blame is intended. Some of the
old who have been given few of life's chances are "so enmeshed in
the daily requirements of life that they don't tend to look much
further. . . . The range of possibilities that are part of the mental
ecology of most just are not there" (Kelly 1987, p. 147). Others
have been so socialized into a certain "voice" that their sense of
self is cemented to expectations of propriety and role.

What is the dynamic in old age that makes freedom more likely then than in the younger years? Barbara Myerhoff suggests a possible answer when she says,

> It is not unusual to find old people who are liminal beings, living beyond the fixed and regulated categories, beyond the constraints of the superego, which can effectively warn against penalties for transgression. Such penalties have diminished bite when the future is short and uncertain. Often, the less future, the less to lose, from the point of view of the individual, and from the point of view of society; often old people are dispensable, their conduct a matter of little consequence, their controls a matter of diminished importance. It may be, then, that the oft-noted but little-studied toughness, fearlessness, idiosyncrasy, and creativity among the elderly in many societies result from this combination of social irrelevance and personal autonomy. (1984, pp. 311-312)

Our argument for the growth of the possibility of freedom in the final stage of life, then, runs like this: to the extent that old age is a *terra incognita*, an uncharted world, a place identified by "mainstream" (i.e., the non-old) society as socially irrelevant and whose inhabitants are dispensable; and to the extent that the events and stages of old age inevitably put one in a kind of marginal existence— to that extent the possibility and challenge of freedom grows in old age.

Once again, however, we affirm that this dimension of spirituality in the last stage of life is intricately interwoven with communities of support and dialogue. The last stage of life has some terrible vulnerabilities. Even in circumstances intended to be very safe, the frail old in some nursing homes will not complain about their care for fear of retaliation. On the other hand, while a specific instance of freedom hardly constitutes a universal argument, I know of a nursing home where the residents voted to have those with dementias kept on the same floor with them. "We wouldn't want to be put away if we got sick that way," they reasoned. "We can put up with a little yelling."

CONCLUSION

I began with a conviction: the last years of life cannot be adequately described without attention to a struggle to keep the human spirit from being overwhelmed by frailty. I described this as a spiritual struggle. It was within this framework that I explored some facets of spirituality and community in the last stage of life. Throughout I have noted the necessary interrelationship of spirituality, community, and the last stage of life.

There is a dimension that belongs in this discussion which has been present only by implication, namely the impact of gender, socio-economic status, birth cohort, and context (including race and ethnicity) on the ways in which one ages with dignity. I know some African-American women in the last stage of life who come each day to a senior center whose programs are chronically short of money because the participants cannot pay. These woman have no income because the people for whom they worked as maids and nannies paid nothing towards pensions and not a cent towards their Social Security. These are people for whom the variables of gender, socio-economic status, context (including race), and birth cohort have had a life-long negative impact.

It is hard to imagine that they have survived. Yet I can report that, in spite of their poverty, in spite of hard lives, these are women of character, of inner beauty, of deep spirituality, women grateful for the good of each day. In spite of years of isolating work, they learned lessons of faith and faithfulness in their churches. Now, without rancor or complaint, they will tell you who they are and Whose they are. I end with their story not because the circumstances of their lives are in any way to be desired or emulated. I raise them up simply to invite your wonder at people who had nothing, but whose presence make us attentive to the centrality of a spirituality grounded in community in the last stage of life.

REFERENCES

Barkan, B. (1995). "The Regenerative Community: The Live Oak living center and the quest for autonomy, self-esteem, and connection in elder-care." In L. Gamroth, J. Semradek, & E. Tornquist (Eds.), *Autonomy in Long-Term Care.* New York: Springer.

Berger, P. (1967). *The Sacred Canopy.* Garden City, NY: Doubleday.

Blythe, R. (1979). *The View in Winter: Reflections on old age*. New York: Penguin.

Cole, T.R., Achenbaum, W.A., Jakobi, P., Kastenbaum, R. (1993). *Voices and Visions of Aging: Toward a critical gerontology*. New York: Springer.

Cole, T.R. (1986). "The 'Enlightened' View of Aging." In T.R. Coles and S.A. Gadow (Eds.), *What Does It Mean To Grow Old*. Durham, NC: Duke University Press.

Friedman, D. (Winter, 1991). "Miracles Every Day." *Inside*.

Healey, S. (1986). "Growing to Be an Old Woman: Aging and agism." In E.P. Stoller & R. C. Gibson (1994), *Worlds of Difference: Inequality in the aging experience*. Thousand Oaks, CA: Pine Forge Press.

Hoffman, M.A. (1985). *The Older We Get . . . An action guide to social change*. Boston, MA: Unitarian Universalist Service Committee.

Hughes, S. (Trans. and Ed.) (1979). *Catherine of Genoa: Purgation and Purgatory; The Spiritual Dialogue*. New York: Paulist.

Kane/Lewis, Producers (n.d.). *Water From Another Time*. Chicago: Terra Nova Films.

Kavanaugh, K. (Trans. and Ed) (1987). *John of the Cross: Selected Writings*. Mahwah, NJ: Paulist.

Laurence, M. (1964). *The Stone Angel*. Toronto: McClelland & Stewart.

Maitland, D.J. (1991). *Aging as Counterculture: A vocation for the later years*. New York: Pilgrim Press.

Midlarsky, E. & Kahana, E. (1994). *Altruism in Later Life*. Thousand Oaks, CA: Sage Publications.

Moody, H.R. (1986). "The meaning of life and the meaning of old age." In T.R. Coles and S.A. Gadow (Eds.), *What Does It Mean To Grow Old*. Durham, NC: Duke University Press.

Moody, H.R. (1995). "The Meaning of Old Age: Scenarios for the future." In D. Callahan, R. ter Meulen, & E. Topinkova (Eds.), *A World Growing Older: The coming health care challenges*. Washington, DC: Georgetown University Press.

Moore, T. (1992). *Care of the Soul*. New York: HarperCollins.

Myerhoff, B. (1984). "Rites and Signs of Ripening: The intertwining of ritual, time, and growing older." In D. Kertzer & J. Keith (Eds.), *Age and Anthropological Theory*. Ithaca, NY: Cornell University Press.

Palmer, P. (1983). *To Know and We Are Known*. San Francisco, CA: Harper & Row.

Seagrim, A.M. (June 27, 1994). "My World Now: Life in a nursing home, from the inside." *Newsweek*, p. 11.

Simmons, H.C. (1988). "Religious Education of Older Adults: A present and future perspective." *Educational Gerontology, 14*, 4.

Simmons, H.C. (1990). "Countering Cultural Metaphors of Aging." *Journal of Religious Gerontology, 7*, 1/2.

Sullivan, E.V. (1984). *A Critical Psychology: Interpretations of the personal world*. New York: Plenum.

Dignity, Cultural Power
and Narrative Redemption:
Aging Male Writers
Confront the Medical System

Robert Disch, MA

INTRODUCTION

The first half of the 1990s witnessed an outpouring of autobiographies describing encounters of ill and aging writers with the medical system, a genre variously referred to as "self stories," "illness stories," or "pathographies" (Hawkins 1993).

In this essay I want to examine three of these works in relation to what established authors have to tell about the nature of dignity, aging, and illness. I have chosen male writers because men generally respond to medical treatment with a naivete I have not found characteristic of female authors. In general, women writers appear less surprised or more "treatment hardened" in their response to the indignities presented by the medical system. The gender-dictated "innocence" or machismo of the males, on the other hand, may have greater value for enlightening us about the relationship between dignity and medical treatment than do illness stories by the more medically sophisticated women.

The Authors

The writers discussed below–Reynolds Price, Paul West and Wilfrid Sheed–share important biographical characteristics (Price 1994,

[Haworth co-indexing entry note]: "Dignity, Cultural Power and Narrative Redemption: Aging Male Writers Confront the Medical System." Disch, Robert. Co-published simultaneously in *Journal of Gerontological Social Work* (The Haworth Press, Inc.) Vol. 29, No. 2/3, 1998, pp. 93-109; and: *Dignity and Old Age* (ed: Robert Disch, Rose Dobrof, and Harry R. Moody) The Haworth Press, Inc., 1998, pp. 93-109. Single or multiple copies of this article are available for a fee from The Haworth Document Delivery Service [1-800-342-9678, 9:00 a.m. - 5:00 p.m. (EST). E-mail address: getinfo@haworthpressinc.com].

West 1995, Sheed 1995). Each struggled to master his craft, endured until his work caught on, became visiting professor or writer in residence at prestigious universities, won prizes and honors and finally earned the esteem of serious readers and professional critics. Then, like the thief in the night, they all were struck by catastrophic illness and the complex meeting with the medical system described in their autobiographies.

In writing about their illnesses, each of the authors attempts, in the words of Reynolds Price, to provide the reader with "an accurate and readable account of a frightening and painful time . . . an honest narrative, a true record of the visible and invisible ways in which one fairly normal creature entered a trial . . . and emerged . . . on a whole new life" (Price, vii).

Significantly, all of the writers elected to forgo their preferred fictional practice to write "non-fiction." This was done to shorten the distance that inevitably emerges between imaginative creation, or "fiction," and the claims of "real" life. Wilfrid Sheed speaks for the others when he writes that he first intended to develop a fictional character "to whom the whole thing *really* happened . . . But in matters of sickness and death you have to put up or shut up. You have to level. Did this happen or didn't it?" (Sheed, 12).

All of the authors were privileged people at the time of illness; none received treatment from an HMO or clinic setting or lacked resources to access medical services. All had strong support from family and friends and could call upon influential connections when necessary. Two were on friendly terms with influential doctors affiliated with the institutions that provided treatment. All, nevertheless, suffered profound challenges to their sense of dignity while undergoing medical care and were required to draw upon internal resources to maintain a sense of selfhood and self-respect.

Two of the writers, Paul West and Reynolds Price, had not previously experienced major illness; but all three, including Sheed, were totally unprepared for the trial that was coming. This sense of lost innocence and discovery gives their writings a universal quality reminiscent of Plato's "Allegory of the Cave." After illness strikes, the writers are dragged into the "light" of knowledge about the modern medical system and the reality of their mortal selves. All interpret this knowledge as significantly altering their fundamental identities. The verbal brilliance with which they describe this process is what separates these books from the ordinary and places them among the important cultural documents of our time.

In the early stages of their enlightenment the writers either assume, or at least hope, that medical treatment will provide a "cure" and return them to the normalcy they had previously enjoyed. None expected to permanently abide in what has been termed the "remission society," an ever-expanding community inhabited by mostly permanent residents. But that is exactly what happened to all of them.

These authors are among the best we have and are accustomed to being treated like the best. At the time of onset all possessed and exercised significant cultural power because they could employ language with singular (or magical) ability. Without warning this creative life process is interrupted and the "narrative" of their lives is "wrecked," as sociologist Arthur W. Frank succinctly put it (Frank 1994, 75 ff).

For a time they cannot write or teach or drink or have sex. What is especially galling, they must accept what others tell them to do. If they aspire to return to the land of the normal, they must follow "doctor's orders." Illness is tolerated by others, according to Talcott Parsons, in so far as the patient submits to the dictates of medical officialdom. A note from the doctor allows the patient to miss school or work, and to stay in bed until recovered. But only if "doctor's orders" are followed (Parsons 1973, Chapters 1 and 2).

Once diagnosed and confronted with the terrifying reality of catastrophic illness, the imagination must begin to create a whole new life; locate the genius within the illness or fall in love with daylight. The writer must construct a new and profoundly different narrative to compensate for the wreck his life story has become.

For all of these authors, the inability to work as a writer is identified as the most devastating of losses, an interruption which impedes recovery. The writers become aware of the extent to which they are self-defined as existing because they write, and not the other way around.

The Encounter

As the disease progresses and treatment attempts to contain or cure it, the writers become increasingly restive and frustrated with the medical system. This process is all too familiar to anyone who has spent much time as a patient and has been recorded in dozens of books and articles (Hawkins 1993).

But for the writers there is both a different and a greater problem than for most of us. They are perplexed and angered at the medical system because it is, above all, a countervailing source of profound power, the power to interpret the human body and to make decisions on ultimate matters of sickness and health, of life and death. And, in the case of the writers, of their ability to write or not write. This stupendous power, so at odds with the inane and sometimes sadistic manner in which medical treatment is often delivered, presents a special problem for people who reap accolades as creators and interpreters of culture. Suddenly, with minimal preparation, the creators are in the hands of people who normally do not know or care what the writer's life-project is about. The doctors are accustomed to interpreting symptoms and applying medical knowledge and technology to cure the patient of disease. In the meeting with the patient, no one ever doubts who *they* are.

The impact on the writers of this imbalance of power is, if not greater, at least qualitatively different than for the average person. In their study, *The Hidden Injuries of Class*, Richard Sennett and Jonathan Cobb concluded that occupational status is highest in the professions that interpret the world to the uninitiated: hence judges, college professors, and doctors rank ahead of bank presidents, corporation executives and stock brokers. Interpretation first, money second, was an important part of their findings.

Perhaps more than any of the occupations Sennett and Cobb studied, the doctors, in charge of interpreting the body and making life and death decisions, and the writers, in charge of interpreting and creating the imaginative life of the society, belong at the top of the list (along with other artists). Certainly the medical profession has gained incredible power since Jenner, Pasteur, Lister, Semmelweis, Fleming and other discoverers gifted to the profession the ability to predictably and consistently prevent, cure or impede a host of devastating illnesses, a recent development in medical history. But in the eyes of the writers, the doctors are seen as little more than conduits for this inherited power, professionals who have "lucked-out" and gained a rich living from the genius of others.

The writers, on the other hand, see themselves as deriving transcendent power from the act of creation itself.

In addition, the writers claim—or have claimed for them by philosophers and scholars from Nietzsche and Matthew Arnold to George Steiner and Harold Bloom—responsibility for the imaginative health of the culture. Meeting in the examination room, these two (understandably) egomaniacal forces are inevitably at odds. Both embrace self-conceptions that empower. The doctors are not accustomed to patients who command the language to ask probing questions and who (naively) expect to receive intelligent replies devoid of condescension. The writers are unprepared for the chronic disrespect toward the patient encountered at all levels of medical practice. Neither profession has much experience playing second fiddle.

But at the time of the encounter it is the writer's dignity (or self-conception) that is at risk. Unlike the doctor, the writer is no longer practicing his profession, though he is certainly collecting valuable information that will be used as soon as he can return to the word processor. The doctor and his entourage, on the other hand, are representatives from the "normal" society. They are in the hospital as part of the medical system, but they are not ill. Worse, far from seeing the creators of the imaginative life of the society on the examination table, the doctors do not accord any special recognition or status to the writer-patient. They certainly do not find the often impractical, dreamy, possibly addicted, maybe even "nutcase" writer to have much to do with anything as important as sustaining civilized existence. The writers, with prizes, accolades and years of success, suddenly find themselves, if not quite bereft, at least highly vulnerable.

REDEEMING NARRATIVES

Surviving Treatment

In *A Whole New Life*, Reynolds Price, an English teacher at Duke University, writes that after experiencing difficulty walking, ". . . I went to a humane physician, an internist at Duke Hospital . . ." (Price, 8). Why humane? The need to identify a doctor as "humane" signals the attitude of the writers in general. Meeting a "humane" doctor following dozens of doctor encounters is thought exceptional enough to be remarked. This humane internist huddles with a neurologist out of the room. Together they inform the writer-patient that he must cancel travel plans and immediately enter the hospital for testing.

Reluctantly Price agrees, entering the hospital on the following morning and experiencing "the usual welcoming session with a sullen admissions clerk . . ." A battery of painful, unanesthetized tests, including nerve-speed probes and a myelogram, are conducted in "a cramped examining room [that] seemed near to exploding with excess light . . ." Price begins to experience a "growing sense" that he

> is being consumed by a single vast live idiot creature concealed throughout this enormous building. The creature has just one blank eye of the keenest focus and not one atom of self awareness or even remorse at its endlessly accumulating knowledge, its power over the building's inhabitants–sick and well–and its impotence or refusal to help them. (Price, 12, 13)

Two days later he is lying on a gurney in a busy hospital corridor wearing "only one of those backless hip-length gowns designed by the standard medical-warehouse sadist . . ." and being "stared at by the usual throng of stunned pedestrians who swarm hospitals round the world . . ." While in this vulnerable position he is told that the tests have revealed a 10-12 inch tumor wrapped around his spinal cord beginning under the hair line. Immediate surgery is recommended. Once the report has been given, the doctors move on, leaving Price and his brother "empty as wind socks, stared at by strangers." (Price, 12, 13).

The initial diagnosis is terrifying; the hallway hubbub in which the bad news is delivered is degrading. What is especially appalling is that the doctors and medical people, emissaries from the "blank-eyed monster," don't recognize the situation as appalling: they just don't get it. They have not a glimmer about the meaning of dignity to a sick or old person, or presumably for any patient. To them it's just a matter of conducting business, wherever and however, on a normally busy day.

To treat what is ultimately diagnosed as a slow-growing malignancy, Price undergoes scalpel surgery and X-ray treatment. Because of the lethal threat posed by the tumor (which Price designates "The Eel"), he is given a lifetime's limit of radiation in a five-week period.

> The presiding radiation oncologist had begun our first meeting by telling me, with all the visible concern of a steel cheese-grater, that my tumor was of a size that was likely unprecedented in the annals of Duke Hospital–some fifty years . . . I wondered *'Does he want me to cheer with personal pride?'* (Price, 41)

While some of the staff and other patients are kind, he never manages

> to mitigate my quick discovery that in my case at least . . . one of the two most grueling brands of cancer treatment . . . would be presided over by a radiation oncologist . . . who gave the unbroken impression . . . of being nothing so much as a nuclear physicist whose experimental subjects were, sadly for them, human beings . . . [the oncologist] . . . saw me as seldom as he could manage. He plainly turned aside when I attempted casual conversation in the halls; and he seemed to know literally no word or look of mild encouragement or comradeship . . . what I wanted and needed badly, from that man then, was the frank exchange of decent concern . . . When did such a basic transaction between two mammals require postgraduate instruction beyond our mother's breast? (Price 50, 56)

Urged by friends to unleash his anger, he finds the doctors unworthy. "True, I felt a certain realistic dread of excess contact with medical doctors, but even my coldest freeze-dried doctor was hardly a fit object of rage–inhumanity is appallingly common in the upper regions of that profession" (Price 55).

With the elite Duke University doctors judged unworthy of authorial rage, Price goes on to finish this part of his painful journey. At the end of his radiation therapy Price finds that the oncologist

> . . . had nothing more to offer by way of human exchange than the patent fact that I'd have to wait now and see what resulted.

Though he didn't define his implications, I understood them to be rapid death or slower total paralysis as the tumor crushed out, one by one, the final crucial nerve connections between my lower back and my brain. . . . When I asked him for practical suggestions of things to do in the interim (I was thinking about exercise, diet or meditation–the last things many American physicians ever speak about), he gave me his blankest look, shrugged and said 'Write the Great American Novel.' (Price, 66, 67)

A friend accompanying Price takes charge: ". . . she stared the oncologist dead in his eye and said, 'He's already written that.'" (Price, 66, 67).

Unsure as I was of her accuracy, I tasted triumph for one hot instant; and we both walked out, me dragging my right leg, leaning on the stout four-footed cane and both of us laughing as we reached the door. (Price, 67)

The triumphant laughter of a man convinced he's dying is sufficient to reestablish the power balance with the one-eyed monster's representative. He will live through the pain, the despair, the suicide fantasies, the paraplegia and regain his writerly existence, a whole new life within a profoundly altered body.

To effect this Price first turns to traditional rehab, which he finds liberating because of "the general absence of doctors." But traditional rehab does nothing to relieve the excruciating pain he has suffered since the surgery and radiation. To deal with the problem, a conference is held between an anesthesiologist and a psychiatrist. Together they determine that he "wasn't insane." The doctors recommend drug treatment that includes methadone. "The Pain Clinic . . . offered me nothing but a handful of drugs that clouded my life for years to come . . . [and] the help of the pain clinic stopped there, where so many American physical problems are grounded by doctors who've blindly or wilfully impoverished their humane intelligence–on prescription blanks" (Price, 99, 108, 109).

Ultimately, Price discovers hypnosis, bio-feedback, imaging, and other alternative methods that successfully contain the immobilizing central pain. This allows him to kick a (by then) two-year-old methadone habit and the narcotized life that went with it.

> Neither of the pain specialists made any mention whatever of the proven survival techniques which at that instant were on hand only yards away from the Pain Clinic . . . I was left to sit and bear central pain with whatever resources my solitary mind could summon in its torpid drugged state. (Price, 109, 112)

Why hadn't he learned of these techniques earlier?

> Despite my years of residence in a university community where some of my friends were medical doctors of world-famed distinction, as a patient I was in most ways an entirely average floater in the crowded wake of disease and its aftermath . . . wasn't I normal in assuming that if likely remedies existed I'd surely be sent right toward them? (Price, 111-112)

This attitude of trust combined with numbed narcotization impeded the discovery of the alternative treatments that ultimately would save his sanity, perhaps his life. By discovering and applying these techniques, he is able to return to the word processor and recover his creative self. Price wonders: if the highly privileged are unable to access dignity-restoring relief from pain in the middle of the Duke Hospital, what chance is there for the "millions less lucky and less well placed who are likewise stuck with the same victim's mute passivity. Most of them live on sheer brute stamina, the body's dogged refusal to quit, till they die in blind torment" (Price 113).

As Price develops into a veteran patient, he realizes that among the hospital staff only a few black nurses see him as a human being:

> By something more than an accidental grace . . . , those women were able to blend their professional code with the oldest natural code of all—mere human connection, the simple looks and words that award a suffering creature his or her dignity.

These nurses were "the only persons . . . who ever asked my opinion of my care—was I being treated well? What else did I need? Certainly no medical doctor ever asked" (Price 132, 133).

At the close of this astonishing work, Price gives his readers guidelines for dealing with catastrophic illness. Among them is the observation that "Nobody–least of all a doctor–can rescue you now, not from the deeps of your own mind, not once they've stitched your gaping wound" (Price, 182). To heal the patient must construct his or her own narrative, one that equalizes and then transcends the arrogance of traditional medicine.

War of Words

Equally as dignity-threatened and as unforgiving as Price is the fiercely verbal Paul West in his book *A Stroke of Genius*. An Oxford graduate familiar with Greek and Latin, West combines linguistic skills and a razor-sharp comic vision to salvage dignity from the assaults of medical treatment and to help comprehend the dimensions of his illness.

In the early stages of recovery from a stroke, while in an ICU, he quickly identifies the use of medical shorthand as an enemy of dignity. As he slowly regains consciousness he becomes aware that he is no longer "Paul West," but rather the ICU's "Atrial Fib."

To cope with the dehumanizing atmosphere of the ICU, he indulges in what he calls his "verbalist's cackle":

> In intensive care [with] whatever energy I could muster, I tried to take an interest in what had happened to me: the pupil of my own mishap, asking the nurse to write out, for me to learn by heart, what propranolol is made of, and heparin, and Coumadin, and quinidine, those promoters of my later life. (West, 37)

Putting to use his knowledge of languages he undertakes a detailed study of the *Physician's Drug Manual*. ". . . I devoured my PDM, discovering that . . . henceforth I was to eschew leafy green vegetables . . . so goodbye, broccoli, spinach, cabbage, and cauliflower. What savorable irony: I had to wait decades for something to come along that would forbid me the foods I loathed" (West, 101).

Soon he is instructing the doctors about the Greek and Latin roots of prescription drugs, lessons that go unappreciated. At one point he learns that quinine, which he takes to alleviate blinking, appears to him to be chemically close to quinidine. "I brought this gem of serendipity to [his doctor] who gave me the look of the savant confronting the half-initiated infidel." This kindly, erudite doctor (who incidentally also earns the sobriquet "humane") had his patience exhausted by the precocious student (West, 104).

The study of the PDM is part of West's growing recognition that he must try to dominate the disease by discovering how much of curative power is in knowing the cause and possible cure of the problem. "To be born is to be transmutable, for better or worse, while awaiting the worst." But "the worst" can be temporarily delayed if the victim can comprehend the nature of the illness and treatment (West, 2).

Later, during an examination by a neurologist, West gives "inventive answers," thinking this would show the doctor that he was "capable of high spirits, was willing to fight back." When the doctor is not amused, West observes: "I upset his professional solemnity, and it did not occur to him that, if there was any solemnity to what was going on, it was mine. All this was about me, not about him or his reputation" (West, 42).

As West masters the jargon surrounding his illness, he tries it out on his doctors, with results as dismal as his pharmaceutical explorations. His appropriation of the professionals' shorthand for fibrillation he finds annoys the doctors: "They didn't like me to call it 'fib'; I was being too familiar with their arcana" (West, 42).

Toward the close of his stay in intensive care, he claims that "I, who had little enough to do with doctors, now began to discover their nature" (West, 43).

> What I, as a wordsmith, [I] especially resented was the way some of these recently graduated sawbones said about my incapacity to describe my symptoms. They made me angry, and in so doing, got for themselves a hyperarticulate account of their own grossness. My version of my symptoms was not simple enough for them to understand, couched in words well within their spectrum of anticipation." (West, 43)

West finds that many doctors display an arrogance similar to that found in the military and among literary theorists of academe. "What is important to keep in focus is the concealed, dissimulated, or even ablated humanity of the doctor concerned." While West is willing to concede that doctors cannot become "too involved or identified with patients," there is nevertheless "no way of dropping out of the species, or the universe, and doctors should get rid of that high-and-mighty manner, of panjandrum hubris" where "elements of [a] secret society . . . mingle with an Inca-like disdain for the masses. Habitude has engendered hebetude, and familiarity overfamiliarity" (West, 46).

Despite disappointing forays into equalizing the doctor/writer power relationship, West intensifies the verbiage when he learns he needs a pacemaker. At one point he is directly warned by a distinguished cardiologist and personal friend that his prosecutorial questioning of the implant surgeon could have undesirable outcomes: "The very search you subject [the surgeon] to may produce just the flaw you fear." Finally West realizes that by . . . Asking questions, you feel less powerless, yet you end up not much wiser or even better informed." Having gained this insight West ends the interrogation and submits to the care of the surgeon (West, 68, 71).

Ultimately he is able to transcend the perceived assaults on his dignity (and his ego) to turn the experience into creation and renewal. Following his stay in the hospital he began "the most sustained period of creativity and reward I had ever known . . . the mind stretched to a new idea never returns to its original dimensions . . ." "All that has happened . . . good and bad . . . is never to be shrugged off . . . I have become what I am, not in spite of what has happened to me, but because of it." Recognizing that "Death is no alternative to anything," he develops a "quiet mania" intended "to get away with as much as I can for as long as I can; tread quietly and applaud my body for its ability to survive" (West, 40, 9, 92).

Hell as Cliche

Wilfrid Sheed, at the beginning of his illness memoir, *In Love with Daylight*, announces that he will write "impersonal non-fiction" "stripped of the armor of fiction . . . ," a decision that reflects the abiding distrust in the Anglo Saxon world for works of the literary imagination (Sheed, 12).

Unlike the other authors under discussion, Sheed had already suffered catastrophic illness: he had polio at age 13 and post-polio syndrome in his mid-fifties. The illness deprived him of the beloved sports he played as a child. Later he will document further losses: sleeping pills and alcohol are foregone because they contribute to suicidal depression; cigars are given up because they may have caused his cancer of tongue and neck; and surgery on the tongue causes diminished ability to salivate, which in turn leads to a loss of the sense of taste.

As for the earlier polio, Sheed had long since grown accustomed to accepting the losses. His adjustment was so complete that people who had known him for years would register surprise when they finally noticed that he walked with a serious limp. He credits his success in adapting to polio and accepting the losses with steeling him for the life and death struggles with addiction, depression, and cancer, a series of catastrophic illnesses that drove him to the brink of suicide. But the crisis that leads to the writing of his book is identified as addiction-depression.

For the modern writer at least, hell may just be another term for medical treatment. Likewise for Sheed. When he is reluctantly forced to concede that abuse of sleeping pills and alcohol are con-tributing factors in his depression, he has no alternative but to subject himself to the rigors of an AA-type treatment program.

Until this point his wrath at the medical system has been muted. The treatment center, he discovers, is a form of hell in cliches:

> In the new world I was about to enter, the assumption was that it was always the truth you were flinching from like a vampire at high noon, and never from just a cliche or, in this case, a shower of cliches, the bane of my profession. (Sheed, 89)

Any criticism of the treatment center's therapeutic language was read as flight from the only "truth" that mattered: that Wilfrid Sheed was an alcoholic with low self-esteem. Sheed's efforts to explain the writer's point of view on the language used in treat-ment–and how it may actually impede healing–was dismissed as nothing more than a form of denial.

At the treatment center, which he dubs the "Happy Valley," the mismatch between the author's fine linguistic sensibility and the cliche-ridden verbiage of the therapeutic milieu, inevitably clash.

The question is, can the writer survive this milieu? Can he take away anything useful from a setting so antithetical to the values of his linguistically structured world view?

In Sheed's case the answer is yes. Through a long and brilliantly narrated process, he comes to fruitful realizations about the nature of treatment, AA and the "faculty" that runs the center.

At first Sheed can only see in the AA treatment program–"One Disease Fits All" as he calls it–an effort to get him to surrender his self-conception (or ego) and submit to the therapeutic cliches. The struggle for Sheed, who is in fact a drug addict but probably not an alcoholic, will be to find a middle ground on which some kind of compromise will be possible, a deal in which he can accept help without suffering further loss of dignity or selfhood:

> Was there any way of just giving up alcohol without becoming a 'type'–either a wistful loser (or 'dry alcoholic' as they're called in the club) or a sleek winner who has given up too much of himself and turned into a Fuller Brush salesman? (Sheed, 91)

A problem for the American writer of Sheed's generation is the awareness that many of the best of his profession, including Nobelists Sinclair Lewis, Eugene O'Neill, William Faulkner, and Ernest Hemingway, were alcoholic or severe abusers for some or all of their lives. From Sheed's point of view, ". . . a child of twelve or forty could see that if you *weren't* on it, *didn't* drink yourself to death, you hadn't a ghost of a chance of making it as a writer" (Sheed, 91).

Accused in group therapy of low self-esteem and indulging in "grandiosity," Sheed argues that artists are in fact different: "I realized that my own self-esteem was usually as good as my last review . . . as with many artists from the best to the bogus, my work was myself . . . and it stood in for all the blows and all the praise, the raspberries and the roses that normal people receive in person. The typical artist . . . [who] barely even takes in compliments that don't relate to his work . . . certainly isn't interested in compliments or insults to his character." Unfortunately the armor provided by identifying as a writer temporarily disappeared when he cannot work at Happy Valley. "Suddenly I was stripped of my alter ego, my stand in. I hadn't worked that morning, and I hadn't wanted to. And just like that I wasn't a writer anymore–but I wasn't anything else either. So okay, I have low self-esteem–tell me what to do about it, and let's get started on it" (Sheed, 115-116).

Like Paul West, Sheed has a natural inclination to spar verbally with the treatment center staff. When he encounters their favorite term, "low self-esteem," he immediately wants to explicate how Dickens and Jane Austen used "self-esteem." And with his novelist's eye he sees the differences among the patients at the Valley and angers because they are all receiving the same treatment. "But what purpose," he wonders, "would be served by ridiculing this battered old faculty" (Sheed, 114).

At first he doesn't consider "a lifetime spent at AA meetings a sufficient inducement to quit drinking." But eventually he sees that, "Like many organizations, Alcoholics Anonymous turns its worst face to the world; in fact, its whole organizational apparatus probably is its worst face, and its spokespeople are its worst voice." But beneath the public facade, he finds a quiet tradition of subversion, resistance and rebellion, often expressed through dark or savage humor. As one long-time AA member explains, AA is composed of "Parrots lecturing to sheep." This subversive aspect of the organization's underside is appreciated by Sheed the writer. And it is this insight that will allow him to continue with the Program, with its flaws and jargon, after he leaves Happy Valley (Sheed, 130, 89-90).

At departure he makes a decision to write "something encouraging and at the same time believable" about his experience. This task is rendered easier than in his former life, dominated as it was by Ativan and alcohol, because Sheed has become drunk on sobriety. "Good grief, sobriety was fairly flooding the switchboard with similes, word associations, and *mots justes*, all tumbling over each other to get into the sundry pieces I seemed to agree to write every time the phone rang." He had become "legally drunk on lucidity and self-satisfaction," armed to survive a coming bout with cancer, "the next act . . . another tragedy . . . a long one this time . . ." (Sheed, 103, 130, 161-162, 172).

CONCLUSION

In *The Coming of Age*, Simone de Beauvoir argued that only engagement with a meaningful project can save us from the despair of old age. Certainly these authors would concur. The one easy moral of their complex tales is that to survive catastrophic illness and loss of dignity it is necessary to have a vivifying project, one that insists upon your presence. All of these writers had this in their lives before, during and after their illnesses. If the main thing in one's life is fighting disease, the prognosis may not be that good.

In the end the authors are not redeemed because they write, but because they want to write, an important distinction. The desire to write is ultimately more important to their recovery than the reality of writing, which reinforces Beauvoir's argument. For these writers only the most horrible physical pain (in the case of Price) or the most despairing depression (in the case of Sheed) can force them to stop writing. But there is no instance in these books in which the writer ever seriously considers giving up writing or of not identifying as a writer.

The biographical traits shared by these writers are likewise inscribed in their illness stories. All at some point portray themselves as abused artists whose creative gifts go unrecognized by the contending power of the healers, specifically by the doctors. While other elements of society may ignore their significance, the writers are unconcerned about most of them. As Sheed put it, it is the critical opinion of his work that defines self-esteem or the lack of it, and not the opinion of some member of Happy Valley's "faculty." But the doctors are too powerful to be that easily dismissed: they too control an interpretative art that will not be ignored.

It is against this power that the writers attempt to reclaim their illness stories, literally wrest them from those cliche mongers and verbal polluters, the medical and therapy establishments. Hence we find Paul West baiting the doctors about the roots of medical terminology and attempting to master the jargon by knowing it better than the professionals, a battle he is destined to lose. In a similar vein, Wilfrid Sheed cannot make progress until he is willing to let go of the ways in which Mr. Pickwick and Jane Austen thought about "self-esteem." Until each is willing to compromise with the countervailing power, West cannot accept his pacemaker and Sheed cannot graduate from the Happy Valley. For Price, less of a verbal antagonist than West or Sheed, the battle with the medical establishment can begin to recede when it is asserted that he has already written the great American novel. The very preposterousness of the claim contributes to ending the battle with the doctors, the only route to victory in the end.

And victory it is for all three of these spiritual travelers, willing and writing their way through various forms of hell to recover their creative selves. All entered the dark wood in their later decades, suffered severe challenges to their sense of dignity, and all came forth to live whole new lives. They wrestled with the demons of self, society and the medical establishment and survived not only with their writerly powers intact but, as these books attest, greatly enhanced.

REFERENCE NOTES

Beauvoir, Simone de. *The Coming of Age.* New York: Warner Paperback Library, 1973.

Frank, Arthur W. *The Wounded Storyteller: Body, Illness, and Ethics.* Chicago: The University of Chicago Press, 1995. In his important study, Frank employs the terms "wrecked narrative" and "remission society."

Hawkins, Anne Hunsaker. *Reconstructing Illness: Studies in Pathography.* West Lafayette, IN: Purdue University Press, 1993. Contains an extensive bibliography of first person illness stories.

Price, Reynolds. *A Whole New Life: An Illness and a Healing.* New York: Plume/Penguin, 1995. Originally published by Atheneum in 1994.

Parsons, Talcott. *Action Theory and the Human Condition.* New York: The Free Press, 1978, chapters 1-3.

Sennett, Richard and Cobb, Jonathan. *The Hidden Injuries of Class.* New York: Knopf, 1973.

Sheed, Wilfrid. *In Love with Daylight: A Memoir of Recovery.* New York: Simon & Schuster, 1995.

West, Paul. *A Stroke of Genius: Illness and Self-Discovery.* New York: The Viking Press, 1995.

The Cost of Autonomy,
the Price of Paternalism

Harry R. Moody, PhD

I once took our 95-year old friend Larry Morris to a hospital emergency room at 2 o'clock in the morning because my wife and I were anxious about shortness of breath and other unexplained symptoms. After going through paperwork and diagnostic preliminaries, the attending physician that night proceeded to explain what might be wrong. After starting a conversation with Mr. Morris, the doctor soon began to speak directly to me, looking in my eyes and talking exclusively for my benefit, treating Mr. Morris as if he weren't present. After a few moments I interrupted to remind the good doctor that Mr. Morris was, true, a bit hard of hearing but was otherwise perfectly capable of understanding the diagnosis. The doctor quickly realized his mistake and immediately began to treat Mr. Morris in a more respectful fashion. He spoke directly to him and asked questions. Later the doctor explained apologetically to me that he hadn't known about the patient's hearing loss: he had

[Haworth co-indexing entry note]: "The Cost of Autonomy, the Price of Paternalism." Moody, Harry R. Co-published simultaneously in *Journal of Gerontological Social Work* (The Haworth Press, Inc.) Vol. 29, No. 2/3, 1998, pp. 111-127; and: *Dignity and Old Age* (ed: Robert Disch, Rose Dobrof, and Harry R. Moody) The Haworth Press, Inc., 1998, pp. 111-127. Single or multiple copies of this article are available for a fee from The Haworth Document Delivery Service [1-800-342-9678, 9:00 a.m. - 5:00 p.m. (EST). E-mail address: getinfo@haworthpressinc.com].

111

simply assumed that Mr. Morris was confused (demented?) because he couldn't understand what was initially said to him. The doctor had addressed me because he wanted to be sure of compliance with the medication prescribed and I looked like the responsible caregiver.

I cite this incident because that transaction in the middle of the night in an emergency room is one which is repeated endlessly in examining rooms, nursing homes, hospitals, and caregiving settings of every kind. The moral truth revealed that night is familiar: every day in countless ways we treat elderly people as somehow less than competent, as children, to be seen but not heard, not addressed directly. Whatever our intentions, we violate their dignity in ways large and small, sometimes with good intentions and sometimes not. But the indignity remains.

This small incident is revealing in another way, too, because the doctor's behavior was not, at least not in any obvious fashion, an instance of paternalism or disregard for autonomy. After all, the doctor that night didn't fail in his obligation of truth-telling; he didn't interfere in another person's life; he didn't override anyone's judgment on behalf of a presumption of beneficence. I cite the incident precisely because it doesn't have the dramatic qualities associated with controversies about the use of physical restraints or psychoactive drugs; with forced institutionalization of the mentally ill; with hospital discharge planning that sometimes shunts elderly people into nursing homes against their will; or with contending claims over voluntary euthanasia and assisted suicide. But small incidents are revealing for what they tell to us about how we should understand debates about autonomy and paternalism in home care and social service settings, and these settings are the central focus of my discussion.

In brief, I want to argue that the overwhelming focus on autonomy in ethical debates is misconceived. My intent is not to attack autonomy as an ideal but to argue for something of even greater importance: namely, dignity. Yes, we should care about autonomy but we should care about it because we care more deeply about dignity and respect in the way we treat people, especially elderly people. I want to move the debate about autonomy and paternalism to a deeper level: namely, to a consideration of the ethics of dignity and the tragic choices we confront if we believe in treating people in the last stage of life with dignity and respect.

AUTONOMY IN CONTEMPORARY ETHICS

The theory of autonomy that prevails in mainstream ethics today is based on the idea that people are mentally competent unless proved otherwise (a presumption of capacity) and that they should make their own decisions unless they decide voluntarily to delegate decision-making power to others (a theory of agency). The starting point for both ideas is a Cartesian (later Kantian) idea that only fully rational, conscious and explicit acts are susceptible to vindication by moral judgment. Acts that are covert, indirect, or otherwise elusive–that are part of the unconscious or social convention, for instance–are somehow inferior, not quite in the realm of moral scrutiny and judgment.

The view that I take is quite the opposite. The approach proposed here is based on what one might call "tacit action" (by analogy to Michael Polanyi's concept of "tacit knowing"). I believe that many acts of "tacit" intervention–for example, accepting help from another person when I am unable to do something for myself–are often best carried out when no attention is explicitly called to the fact that help is needed or that help is rendered. In collaborative tacit action both parties may very well give each other a "wink and a nod": that is, they implicitly "agree" not to mention what's going on, as sociologist Erving Goffman has revealed in many studies. Actions can be voluntary without being explicitly acknowledged.

There are many times, in fact, when we should go further: not merely do we evade attention or avoid being explicit but we may be well advised to distract attention–for example, by humor–so as not to look directly at something degrading or humiliating that is going on. For instance, if a person is incontinent and soils himself and we have to clean it up, we may intervene but don't have to dwell on the obvious facts. On the contrary, we act with greater ethical sensitivity when we *don't* make things explicit. Similarly, when a mentally frail individual forgets names, we are well-advised to become "co-conspirators" by shoring up the facade of memory and rationality which are so crucial to maintaining dignity. Acting this way is a means of sustaining dignity in the face of assaults that can be demeaning and destructive of respect when they are viewed directly or acknowledged by others.

Now much of what has just been said might strike many people as obvious: it is nothing more than what is called politeness and delicacy. But what is being proposed here under my category of "tacit action" will not be easily accepted by the canons of contemporary ethics. In fact, the argument offered in this chapter is entirely the *opposite* of the one prevailing in the mainstream of contemporary bioethics. Mainstream ethics would have us believe that *only* when someone explicitly and formally delegates consent to another is it proper to interfere in someone else's life. Without explicit and voluntary delegation, interference is justified only when another person has lost mental capacity and even then, on prevailing assumptions, we are obliged to act in accordance with some doctrine of "substituted judgment"–in effect, sustaining the fiction that agency alone, not paternalistic intervention, is involved in the intervention. Only as a last resort–say, when a patient is unconscious and when that patient's intentions and history are utterly unknown–only then are we justified in using our own judgment ("best interest") as a standard based on beneficence to guide intervention.

I have drawn as sharp a contrast as I can between my own account of "tacit action" and what stands as the dominant paradigm in bioethics because I believe a great deal is at stake in deciding which account is correct. If autonomy is the supreme principle, the "gold standard" for ethical correctness, then all acts of intervention, tacit or not, will be viewed with suspicion. The burden of proof is on anyone, professional or family member, who would intervene for the sake of someone else's good: the classic definition of paternalism.

Practitioners in geriatric care professions today face a nearly unanimous consensus on this point: the entire evolution of juridical and ethical thinking over the past three decades is based on certain core assumptions–that explicit is better than implicit, that autonomy takes precedence over paternalism, that agency is acceptable but interfering is not, and so on. Our common language of ethics–of "enlightened opinion"–has come to validate autonomous decision-making to such a degree that people whose mental or physical frailty prevents them from acting independently face a difficulty: do they try to act in accordance with this dominant ideal of autonomy or do they only pretend to act this way and suppress inconvenient facts about social transactions inconsistent with this ideal? Do we continue to sustain actions that promote dignity by a kind of denial that the emperor has no clothes? Finally, how are we to construct an ethics of dignity that makes sense of the conflict between autonomy and paternalism in the care of frail elderly people?

THE ETHICS OF AGENCY

I want to begin the effort to construct an ethics of dignity at what may seem a surprising starting point: namely, the ethics of treatment of the dead. Let me ask a question: Can we be agents for the dead and can we act to carry out the interests of the dead? It is an interesting point that, according to the American law of libel and slander, the dead have no interests. That is, we cannot libel the dead, even if we utter or publish false or derogatory statements in wanton and malicious disregard for the truth. Willful falsehoods may be despicable, but not actionable: we cannot be sued for libeling the dead because, in American law, the dead have no interests.

But if it's true that the dead do not have interests, then how are we to act in carrying out the intentions of the dead for disposition of their property? The answer of course is to follow their last will and testament, if one is at hand. If a will is not available, then other standards apply. Now, if we don't have any testamentary evidence, then we rely on some very general standard—what a "rational person" could be presumed to do. If the dead did have interests, then such actions of probate could be said to be relying on a "best interest standard," which is actually what we do in the case of intestate disposition of a will when we lack any particular knowledge of the intentions of the deceased.

But except for those who die intestate, we normally apply a "substituted judgment standard" when we look to a will and rely on an executor to carry out the intent of that will. An executor thus becomes an agent who, acting with fiduciary responsibility, tries faithfully to interpret and carry out the intent of the deceased. If we doubt whether an agent has acted properly, we can always appeal to a court of law. But, unless our appeal is purely on procedural grounds, we make that appeal based on some argument deriving from substituted judgment, some interpretation of the "real will."

Let us think more carefully about the role of an executor, then, as an agent and let us consider more deeply the moral role of agency as such. Why do we ever need an agent? We need an agent in a situation where we are unable to act on behalf of our interests, a case that seems to apply preeminently in the case of the deceased. Then what about this idea that the dead don't have any interests, as suggested by libel law? Perhaps they don't, but the living do have interests in the memory of the dead. As long as we are among the living we also have an interest in who will be benefited by disposition of property when we ourselves are dead. So, from either a utilitarian or deontological standpoint, we all have an interest in maintaining intact the institution of promise-keeping and an interest in fulfilling promises made to dispose of property in accordance with the wishes of the deceased.

We might say that carrying out the will of the deceased is a paradigm case of *guardianship* on behalf of someone who is vulnerable: the dead need protection because they are completely vulnerable, they can't do anything at all to carry out their will. We the living are in a position to carry out promises made to them. Moreover, we recognize that in the fulfillment of promises, as in the protection of the vulnerable, we touch on the core of ethical obligation, on qualities that make us human.

We might say that acting as a "perfect agent" means to act in accord with a subject's "real will." But action in accord with another's intention is not the same thing as respecting others as long they retain competency to act on their own. On the contrary, interfering with another person's freedom, whether to promote actual best interest or to fulfill someone's (putative) real will, is ipso facto a violation of respect: that is, we are not treating that person with the standard of dignity. Hence, the widespread revulsion against paternalism, even if it is autonomy-enhancing paternalism. Every act of interference comes at a price, invariably diminishing dignity. Even acts in perfect fulfillment with another person's intention, do not diminish this threat to dignity.

A THOUGHT EXPERIMENT

To see why this is so, consider the following thought experiment. Imagine that experts in quantum electrodynamics have invented a machine for reading thoughts and simultaneously predicting events in the near future. By using this new machine, it will be possible to discern what a person's "real will" is and foresee what that person will do in the next moment to carry out that intention. Imagine further that a friendly party possessing this thought-reading machine interferes with my actions to warn me about doing something foolish or acting "out of character." What will be my reaction to this intervention by the friendly party? I reply that it would probably be a mixture of gratitude–for preventing a disaster–along with outrage–for violating my dignity and autonomy.

But wait: Does this intervention actually violate my autonomy? It isn't clear that it does so at all. After all, I still retain the ability to disregard warnings given to me. My freedom has not been curtailed. Of course we might say that my privacy has been invaded by the use of the telepathy machine, and therefore my dignity has been assaulted. But this is another way of saying that perfect knowledge of someone else's real will is ipso facto a violation of dignity. Ah, but perfect knowledge is supposed to be the highest standard for substituted judgment, which is our way of showing respect for people. So we have a contradiction. This thought experiment has already shown us something important: namely, a deviation, a contradiction, between the ethics of agency and the ethics of dignity. The fact that no one has limited my freedom of action and even the fact that the interference was totally in keeping with my real will in no way diminishes the assault on dignity.

We can push the point even further. Suppose that earlier I myself have *voluntarily* agreed to rely on the telepathy machine, perhaps for good prudential reasons. Will voluntary agreement in any way lessen my shock and dismay at having my intentions and future actions preempted by the telepathy device? No, the assault on dignity would be the same. From this thought experiment it is clear that agency, even "perfect" agency, by itself is not a necessary or sufficient condition for respecting someone else's dignity. And the opposite is true as well. The incident of the emergency room doctor's treatment of Larry Morris showed that it is quite possible to diminish someone's dignity without involving questions of agency or autonomy.

But this line of argument suggests an important question: Is *any* form of paternalistic intervention acceptable? Are we not running a risk of assaulting people's dignity even under the most stringent conditions (substituted judgment, voluntary agency, and so on)? Strong advocates for autonomy—and there are many—will take a hard line on this question, arguing that autonomy is always to be presumed and promoted, except under the most extreme circumstances. Their argument makes paternalism something akin to martial law: an expedient adopted only as an emergency measure with carefully circumscribed limitations. On this view, paternalism is not "normal" for ethical behavior, especially among those, like frail elders, whose dignity may be precarious for all kinds of reasons. This line of argument seems to drive a final nail into the coffin of paternalism.

PATERNALISM IN LIFESPAN PERSPECTIVE

But is such a hostile attitude toward paternalism as an "abnormal" regime finally justified? Perhaps it is not if we look at ethics from a lifespan development perspective. We might argue this point starting with the paradigm instance of paternalism, the case from which the very word "paternalism" originates: namely, parental intervention in the lives of children. One reason why parental paternalism is acceptable of course is because of limited mental capacity. But from a developmental standpoint it is acceptable because a child exhibits trust (a kind of tacit consent) and because the child seems to accept intervention by the parent as an act of love. The child has trust because of prior love from the parent, and that love remains a necessary, though not sufficient, element for human development.

Though there is much to be said for rehabilitating an "ethic of care," love and care are not the whole story. To say that love is not enough is here more than a cliche because it reminds us, as Kant would insist, that any best interest-standard—"happiness" in Kant's terminology—is only a partial and imperfect yardstick for acknowledging, and developing, our full humanity. Along with love, dignity and respect are crucial to human development over the life cycle, in childhood as in old age. It is not yet clear what an ethic of dignity would require of us, but the hint of an answer can be found by attending closely to the intertwining of love and respect in the paternalistic relation of parents to children.

Understanding the changing dynamic of paternalism, respect, and non-interference in child development is crucial in order to think about the ethics of professional practice with frail elderly clients and in order to make sense of debates about autonomy and paternalism. To imagine a version of paternalism grounded in the protection of dignity and the promotion of autonomy is not to imagine a contradictory ideal. On the contrary it is a very practical strategy, even if that ideal is difficult to practice, as every successful parent, and caregiver, will testify.

The need for respect, for dignity, is just as important as the need for love, and there is an inevitable tension between these two needs. At a point early in the child's life, the child will begin to crave, to need, a measure of respect: that is, non-interference. "I can do it myself," cries the toddler, feeling in some inchoate way that "doing it myself" is a gesture aimed at claiming respect. The sensitive parent will understand the gesture as such. But learning to balance love and respect is not easy. Non-interference can be difficult for a parent because it may seem like a rejection of parental love, and this dialectic of intimacy and detachment remains with us over the life cycle. Total non-interference is not desirable because it represents only a minimalist definition of respect and dignity, and this is where much contemporary ethics has gone wrong. We have been able to imagine an ethics of strangers, but not an ethics of intimacy, and have therefore polarized respect and love. What is called for is an ethics of intimacy that also includes dignity and respect, even elements of detachment, as part of the developmental process.

We are right to be wary of non-interference as a supreme ideal just as we are right to be way of all-consuming love as barometer of the quality of relationships. In relationships and in caregiving in particular, non-interference can serve as a mask for indifference or the detachment of a stranger: "Don't get involved," we say to ourselves passing by tragedies unfolding on a busy street. But detachment and isolation do not imply respect or acknowledgment of dignity: we do not respect the beggar by simply turning away. The ethics of intimacy and the ethics of strangers belong to different worlds of discourse. Substituting the detachment of a stranger (non-interference) will not achieve respect for dignity under the conditions of intimacy involved in day-to-day caregiving for frail elderly people.

We learn something important here by thinking about the ethics of non-interference over the complete human life cycle. What parents of growing children, from toddlers to adolescents, need to work so diligently to achieve is a hard-won style of non-interference. If non-interference is too easy to achieve–if it comes in a form Dietrich Bonhoeffer called "cheap grace"–then it is not the right kind of non-interference at all. The non-interference to strive for is based on continuing care and concern, a care that can support a parent's voluntary detachment from the growing child because of abiding faith that the child will one day achieve true autonomy and adulthood. From the day a child takes a first step in learning to walk, this fundamental pattern of care and detachment, of love and respect, is at work. It plays itself out in the relationship of parent and child and it appears again in the last stage of life.

The tragedy of human life is that, in old age, we have the opposite process unfolding over time. As time goes on the child acquires more and more autonomy, both physical and psychological. But the elderly person over time exhibits less and less autonomy, either on the physical plane (frailty) or on the psychological plane (dementia). Looking at the life cycle as a whole, then, we witness two opposing trajectories: one of growth, the other of decline, a parallel long noted by the poets: e.g., "In my end is my beginning" (T.S. Eliot, *The Four Quartets*).

But to see life merely as a mirror image of two halves joined together is not the whole story and may be quite misleading. Gerontologists tell us that an overriding principle for "successful aging" is not denial but a strategy called "decrement with compensation." What can this strategy tell us about the dialectic of autonomy and paternalism?

Signs of diminishing autonomy in advanced age are clear enough. But where is the compensation? The answer is to be found in an ethical idea of dignity, in acts that treat other people in accordance with neither a best-interest nor a substituted judgment standard, but in accordance with a hard-won ideal of respect.

To see casual parallels in repetitions of dependency across the life cycle–for instance, to see old age as a "second childhood"–is to risk falling into a dangerous trap that can lead to infantilizing the elderly, as happens in some nursing homes and families. On the other hand, to deny parallel patterns of dependency is to forget the meaning of the riddle of the sphinx in the Oedipus story or else to interpret the sphinx's query in the most superficial fashion–which is exactly what the young Oedipus himself did the first time around. A superficial reading of dependency risks making us oblivious to our common human fate: we were all once dependent, we will be so again, and we are so in manifold ways even at this moment. The blindness of adulthood is an intoxication with the illusion of independence: misreading of the life cycle which Oedipus learned to recognize only in old age, as Sophocles shows us in *Oedipus at Colonnus*, that often forgotten third play of his great trilogy.

Perpetuating narcissistic illusions of independence–including non-interference–carries tremendous moral risks for a culture that idolizes independence and autonomy in every sphere of life, as ours does. Denial of dependency overlooks sources for dignity and respect in the structure of human development itself, including the last stage of life with its own psychological task, as Erik Erikson put it, of "ego integrity," surely a powerful invocation of dignity.

To respect the dignity of age requires more of us than "non-interference," or just leaving people alone. Libertarianism is no answer either to social policy or professional practice in an aging society. Caregiving for frail elderly people calls for cultivating a kind of paternalism quite different from the style appropriate for young children: a paternalism that veils itself, and in that way preserves dignity, while at the same time acting to promote the highest possible autonomy on the part of the subject. A standard of the "least restrictive alternative" enunciated in the legal doctrine of autonomy has its validity here, even if it is not the whole story.

COURTESY AS POSITIVE LIBERTY

The whole story must include both positive and negative aspects of relatedness: of "interference," on the one hand, and "detachment" on the other. This idea is not new: Isaiah Berlin distinguished between positive and negative concepts of liberty. Negative liberty is, roughly, the ideal of non-interference as a condition for respecting someone's dignity. "Don't tread on me": that ideal is familiar enough from the U.S. Constitution to John Stuart Mill and to the libertarian streak so pronounced among today's aging Baby Boomers.

But what about positive liberty? For frail elders, positive liberty means a form of intervention that shores up elements of the self threatened by age, illness or frailty. Respecting a person's dignity in this way will often mean sustaining certain fictions or illusions. Consider the case of the Alzheimer's patient who was introduced to company by his wife in the following fashion: "This is Henry. Henry was a lawyer." Upon hearing this Henry interrupted, saying, "No, I *am* a lawyer."

What Henry is claiming here is the dignity of historical selfhood, the honor of his prior (and lifelong) professional identity. Far from being an abstraction (e.g., "personhood"), such a claim of dignity is bound up with a self now perhaps vanished but supremely worthy of memory and respect, just as we cherish the memory of the dead and just as we show respect for dead bodies. For the living, the challenge of showing respect is more subtle. The way we label people, or speak to them, constitutes part of the realm of positive liberty, part of those myriad transactions that sustain the self and make possible human relationships.

At its most minimal, positive liberty is a kind of politeness or courtesy in human society. Now politeness and courtesy are subjects almost never discussed in contemporary ethics, presumably because people find such behavior a trivial matter or an item of social convention (e.g., Miss Manners). But trivial this subject is not. On the contrary, courtesy is a matter of the highest ethical and even spiritual importance: in medieval chivalry, among both Christians and Muslims, courtesy was an integral aspect of a sublime vision of human virtue. But we barely know what to make of such ideals today. There are other, more pressing puzzles that call for understanding. For instance, in more prosaic and contemporary terms, it is not at all easy, in a multicultural world, to know just how to treat others with politeness and due consideration, and it has never been easy to balance truth-telling with courtesy.

A far deeper problem today is that courtesy and politeness, as cultural ideals, simply go against the leading moral shibboleths of our age, as even casual viewing of daytime TV will convince anyone. Instead of courtesy, we tend to favor sincerity and directness. When it comes to the failings of others, instead of discretion, we favor maximum publicity. We want "sunshine" laws instead of secrecy from elected leaders. We believe that if people have something to hide, then there is something morally suspect about them. In short, nothing is to be hidden or protected.

This dominant cultural ethos is more significant, in ethical terms, than snickering about daytime TV talk shows: it manifests itself in styles of clothing (informal), relations between parents and children (relaxed), assumptions about political deliberation (televised), and in a host of other ways. The historical roots of these tendencies are far deeper than contemporary mass media. Americans as a people have always favored informality and directness, and contemporary culture only takes this tendency to an extreme. America, as a political society that originated in revolt against hierarchy and royalty, may always find traditions of courtesy to be suspect.

One of the most important of contemporary ideals, dominant since the time of Rousseau, is the imperative of sincerity or transparency in all social relationships. In the literature of ethics, this ideal of sincerity is enunciated under the obligation of truth-telling. It is here that we confront the deepest tensions between contemporary moral demands of truth-telling and traditional norms of courtesy and discretion. Truth-telling, as anyone knows, can easily be an instrument of profound disrespect, even insult. To say out loud, to someone's face, what we privately think can be a moral outrage, quite the opposite of a moral obligation.

With many situations of frailty in old age, truth-telling presents a serious moral dilemma. For example, if an elderly person is utterly unable to dress himself, or fails to remember names in a conversation, then perhaps the courteous, the most respectful thing to do is to maintain the illusion of capacity, to gloss over behavior that signals loss of capacity. This is not a matter of "lying," as if lying and truth-telling were a simple moral dichotomy. It is a matter of what we might call "cognitive prosthetics"–providing social conventions that smooth over another person's failings, that put someone else at ease, which is after all the deepest definition of politeness. All of social life is made possible by subterfuge of this kind.

Now putting the matter this way underscores just how far contemporary ethics misunderstands the moral dilemmas of caregiving with the frail elderly. The dominant model in bioethics tells us that truth-telling and autonomy are the supreme touchstone for judging action toward others. We are urged to everything possible to sustain a frail older person's autonomy, because, at least in mainstream American culture, independence is crucial to self-respect and dignity. But, perhaps fortunately, we also routinely act in ways to sustain the fiction of autonomy, even where the physical or psychological capacity for it has vanished. We act often enough, in other words, with appropriate politeness and kindness, rightfully failing to confront other people with what would be insulting truths because we prefer to sustain their dignity. We are right to do so, but contemporary ethics gives us a bad conscience about this subterfuge and, still worse, fails to give us direction on how to reconcile competing versions of human dignity.

ETHICAL DILEMMAS IN ALZHEIMER'S

I want to expand on this last idea and also extend the discussion of paternalism and autonomy by looking at one particular problem that arises in caregiving with frail elderly people. That is the problem of truth-telling in cases of a dementing illness such as Alzheimer's Disease. A number of cases of this kind are described in the classic volume *The 36-Hour Day*, but here I want to look at one case study cited by James and Hilde Nelson in their recent book on ethical issues in Alzheimer's Disease.

The Nelsons discuss the case of a couple named Roy and Marie who are coping with the insidious onset of Alzheimer's in Marie. Some of the changes happening to Marie have caused Roy to reexamine his ideas about human life and, in particular, the idea of dignity.

Not long after Marie was diagnosed with Alzheimer's, Roy visits an Alzheimer's respite care program because he recognizes that some time in the future that program might prove necessary. Through a window Roy watches the group participants singing "You are My Sunshine" while they are swaying back and forth to the music. He recognizes that they are enjoying the experience, but their enjoyment bothers Roy because this childish pleasure seems to be a kind of degradation, a loss of dignity, that he cannot accept as the future prospect for a proud woman like Marie. But then in thinking about this prospect Roy has a revelation, a moment of insight: is it possible that dementia *doesn't* actually destroy our dignity, that it doesn't–perhaps can't–rob us of essential humanity? Is it possible, Roy, wonders, that we have the wrong idea of what it means to be human?

The Nelsons go on to elaborate this point: "Many of us tend to blend our mental images of 'dignified person' with our images of 'productive, highly competent person,' forgetting, perhaps, that none of us start out this way" (p. 118). The authors have struck an important chord, here, a theme that Steven Post discusses in his book on ethical issues in Alzheimer's Disease: namely, the fact that we live in a "hyper-cognitive" culture, so much so that any deviation from full mental capacity, from complete rationality and autonomy, is regarded as a fall from "personhood," from human dignity.

In this case study, Roy goes on to speculate that perhaps loss of mental competency isn't a cause for deep humiliation but is, instead, part of a large human story, a life narrative, that can happen to any of us. Instead of judging the respite activity group according to a preconceived idea about dignity, Roy's meditation on the multiple meanings of dignity gives him a new way of accepting Marie and their life together at a time when her dementia is worsening. Becoming more self-reflective about the meaning of dignity, Roy is thus able to be more calm and collected, less anxious and agitated, and he transmits his wider vision to Marie in the way he treats her. Perhaps in the very act of reflecting on a deeper idea of dignity, Roy has found a way of treating Marie with the respect and dignity she needs.

But the story is not over so quickly, and a happy ending is not so easy to achieve. There is a tragic choice involved in this deeper understanding of dignity and of the responsibility it entails. The Nelsons discuss another feature of caregiving: namely, how to enable a person suffering from dementia to preserve the fiction of autonomy and responsible behavior even after reaching a point where cognitive deterioration makes that impossible. In the case of Roy and Marie, we learn how Roy has made arrangements with local merchants and then gives Marie checks stamped "void" to pay for the hairdresser, the butcher, and so on in order for she to maintain the illusion of independent action.

The problem here is that Roy's subterfuge is at odds with living honestly. On the positive side, Marie gets to maintain, longer than she might have, a feeling of autonomy, a belief in her own capacity even when she is no longer in a position to distinguish what's going on. But on the other side, there is a tragic loss in this way of treating Marie:

> . . . without knowing it, Marie may have lost something else she had always prized: the kind of honesty that had consistently been a part of her relationship with Roy. In exchange for receiving the *impression* that she had kept her adult status, she may have lost the *reality* of being treated with the dignity and respect to which an adult is entitled. (p. 125)

But this is not the only way of looking at the situation. One can think of "dignity" not as an isolated transaction but as a part of the whole, as a feature of a wider relationship: a reflection of Marie's entire history creatively expressed in ways not captured by the single dimension of momentary "honesty." The Nelsons feel compelled to argue that by engaging in this deception, even though Marie never learns of the deception, Roy is not "honoring her dignity or treating her with the respect that is her due . . . " (p. 126). The problem here is that treating someone with "dignity" or "respect" is a multidimensional phenomenon: it cannot be reduced to the single dimension of truth-telling, important as truth-telling may be.

What needs to be recognized, as the Nelsons generally do throughout their book, is that the ethics of behavior toward those with dementia inevitably involves tragic choices. It is not just that certain competing values–beneficence, justice, and autonomy, for instance–cannot all be maximized simultaneously. It is rather that the *same* value–dignity–will be compromised one way or another however Roy comes to treat Marie–whether with honesty or with subterfuge.

Further, this problem arises not only in extreme situations of action toward people who are cognitively impaired. In normal, everyday transactions with people, common politeness and courtesy routinely require us to engage in subterfuge of all kinds. Certain acts of subterfuge do involve disrespect, loss of trust, and threats to human dignity; and we are rightly warned to be on guard against the corrosive influence of falsehood. But other acts of subterfuge preserve trust and mutual confidence that are maintained only as long as we avoid brutal honesty that can damage dignity.

We return, in the end, to the primacy of dignity and, even more, to the mystery and the tragic choices it entails. What contemporary ethics needs most is not to abandon hard-won ideals of autonomy and human rights–the precious legacy of the Enlightenment–but to temper those ideals with a perspective suppressed by the progressivist ideology of the Enlightenment: namely, an understanding of tragedy and of the way in which human dignity can thrive even under tragic circumstances. By the last act of *Oedipus* or *King Lear*, the hero, even in reduced circumstances, is not less but more human, more endowed with grandeur and dignity. And the same, we may hope, can be true for the last act of life itself.

In caring for the frail elderly, what caregivers need to hear is what they already know in their hearts: that autonomy has its cost, that paternalism has its price, that there are no easy answers, and that applied ethics at its best will acknowledge and show respect for their struggle, which is itself a part of our dignity. What ethical thinking about old age can do is to remind us of tragic choices and, even more, assure us of the realistic hope for dignity at the end of life.

Assuring Dignity
in Means-Tested Entitlements Programs:
An Elusive Goal?

Sia Arnason, MSW

. . . Basic income support and protected medical care for older people, provided in ways that protect dignity and enhance social solidarity, are critical goods that must be in the forefront of any discussions. These moral values ought not to be eclipsed . . .[1]

INTRODUCTION

The protection of the infirm and the impoverished as a fundamental responsibility of government was first enacted into law in Europe when the Elizabethan Poor Laws adopted the concept of parens patriae through the establishment of almshouses, orphanages and hospices for the sick. These early public programs in Britain were the first "safety-net" programs designed for the disadvantaged who could not help themselves: the feeble-minded, orphans, the sick, and the aged. The Poor Laws were based on "an ethic that held as sacrosanct the proposition that hard work, self-denial, and self-discipline would provide serenity, if not happiness, in this life and ensure moral and even spiritual progress towards the next."[2]

[Haworth co-indexing entry note]: "Assuring Dignity in Means-Tested Entitlements Programs: An Elusive Goal?" Arnason, Sia. Co-published simultaneously in *Journal of Gerontological Social Work* (The Haworth Press, Inc.) Vol. 29, No. 2/3, 1998, pp. 129-146; and: *Dignity and Old Age* (ed: Robert Disch, Rose Dobrof, and Harry R. Moody) The Haworth Press, Inc., 1998, pp. 129-146. Single or multiple copies of this article are available for a fee from The Haworth Document Delivery Service [1-800-342-9678, 9:00 a.m. - 5:00 p.m. (EST). E-mail address: getinfo@haworthpressinc.com].

129

The notion that poverty is somehow a result of personal failure continues to play a dominant role in the distribution of wealth in the United States, the development of public policies for the poor, and the public perception of shame, failure, and stigma associated with the receipt of public entitlements that are means-tested. The negative connotations are of such magnitude that many Americans do not apply for public benefits, even in the face of serious poverty.

Social insurance programs tend to have social and economic objectives (the moral economy of aging). As Lawrence Thompson points out:

> . . . the social protection objectives include treating people with dignity and respect, assuring complete coverage, equitable distribution of costs and benefits, and operating efficiently to lower overhead. The objectives important to promoting a healthy economic environment include encouraging individual saving and work effort, fostering government fiscal responsibility, and facilitating smooth market functioning . . .[3]

The relationship between the two major objectives is not a smooth one and social protection was not always seen as a public good. In the United States the development of a social insurance program for the aged in the early decades of this century was initially heavily criticised: the idea was branded "a counsel for despair"; proponents were considered having "Bolshevik" tendencies; and its beneficiaries were called "State Parasites."[4] However, the stock market crash of 1929, and the Depression that followed, changed public attitudes and the stage was set for the development of social insurance programs for the elderly poor and the unemployed.

When the Roosevelt administration first started planning for a social insurance program, it studied twenty-two European and six non-European countries that had social insurance systems. Roosevelt vetoed the idea of using general tax revenues to finance the program. "We must not have a dole—even in the future" he reportedly said. Instead, a payroll tax mechanism was designed to ensure that a future President and Congress could not reduce or even repeal Social Security because it is an entitlement based on a specific "earnings record."[5] As a government poster of the 1930s proclaimed: "Old Age Should Be The Harvest Of A Fruitful Life." And, Social Security was never intended to be the sole source of income for older persons–on the contrary, Social Security was designed to be one leg of a three-legged stool, the other legs consisting of private savings and pension income.

Today, the Social Security program is a popular program on which millions of Americans rely for income support. Social Security is of course not only an insurance program against poverty in old age, it also offers benefits to the disabled (of any age), the widowed and other survivors, and dependents of its beneficiaries.

POVERTY IN RETIREMENT

- Is impoverishment in old age an assault on personal dignity?
- To what extent is there "personal fault?" Does it matter?
- To what extent does it place one far from the mainstream?

The Social Security program reduced the incidence of poverty among older Americans greatly; it is said that without it the income of 50% of older Americans would fall below the poverty line. But the Social Security program, or the safety net programs that followed it, did not eliminate poverty among older Americans. Poverty in old age, more than 60 years after the enactment of the Social Security Act and 25 years after the enactment of Medicare, is not unusual and it is frequently caused by the high cost of long term care. In New York State the average cost of nursing home care ranges from $60,000 to more than $90,000 per year. As a result, even middle class Americans are likely to become eligible for Medicaid, the health insurance for the poor, after having to "spend down" their assets on home or nursing home care.

Of course, other factors contribute to the significant proportion of elders who experience poverty in old age: *widowhood* (especially for older women who tend to outlive their husbands and who don't have a substantial work history of their own); *ethnicity* (very substantial proportions of elderly African or Hispanic Americans experience poverty in old age), *immigrant status*, and *inflation* (personal savings are generally not adequate to complement Social Security and pension benefits and the three-legged stool of the 1930s has become wobbly over time. Today, many Americans need *a four-legged chair, rather than a three-legged stool, when their frailty requires home care or nursing home care,* with the fourth leg consisting of public entitlements for long term care).

Indeed, an analysis of Long Term Care needs and enrollment, based on the data from the 1989 Long Term Care Survey, notes that at the time data were collected, 19% of community residents were recipients of Medicaid; however, 59% of community residents not on Medicaid would be eligible for it immediately upon nursing home entry.[6]

THE PERSONAL EXPERIENCE
OF POVERTY IN OLD AGE

Poverty for "the newly-poor-in-old-age" is different from poverty caused by a natural disaster or war, it strikes people one at a time (instead of whole groups) and terminates their membership in the middle class. Poverty in old age is not temporary, it lasts until death and drastically alters the familiar trajectory of the working, self-sufficient life; it brings with it feelings of regret, shame and personal blame (invariably questions arise about what could have been done differently); and it frequently requires that adult children offer financial and other assistance to their elders instead of the other way around. Intergenerational caring is taking place today in unprecedented ways, according to the Public Policy Institute of the American Association of Retired Persons: "... in 1989, almost three quarters of severely disabled older persons received home care entirely from family members or other unpaid caregivers ..."[7]

The process of acknowledging and then documenting personal poverty is a major obstacle for most applicants and is invariably seen as shameful, stigmatizing and demeaning. When applying for public benefits, documentation requirements cover a range of very personal, almost intimate, questions that never needed to be shared with others during the applicant's working years. Such questions include: verification of the size and source of income and the size and source of assets; an explanation of recently spent "significant sums" (usually $500 or more) and documentation that full value was received; household composition and the source and degree of support received from others; and if destitute, an explanation of one's means of support in the weeks prior to the application date.

THE TWO FACES OF DIGNITY

Most Americans take pride in the economic security they are able to create for their families–financial self sufficiency defines them and places them squarely in the American middle class, a group much celebrated in American rhetoric, and sets them apart from the other group, those who do not contribute their "fair share" and instead are a drain on the public coffers, the "state parasites" of another time. Furthermore, financial security also offers an opportunity to leave something behind for the next generation, and, leaving a legacy does not only insure the well-being of future generations, it also may offer a semblance of immortality.

Dictionaries offer definitions of dignity that celebrate qualities such as nobility of bearing, behavior, and stature; or that reflect the stuff from which "dignitaries" are made, such as power, control, and authority. These positive attributes are qualities we can recognize even when we cannot easily define them. These comprise the public face of dignity. But the other side of dignity–those essential qualities that belong to the self or humanity–are even less easily defined.

When asked about the human qualities which are created over a lifetime, some will refer to dignity in terms of a life well-lived; a sense of self-respect or self-worth; others will mention satisfaction borne from independence; having conducted oneself according to celebrated values; having contributed to society; having been able to control ones life and exercise autonomy; or finally, to live by an inner light that is respected by others.

Dignity, in short, has two faces. It is both a private affair that "shines from the inside out" and it is also a public validation by others through behavior and communication, including public policies that distribute scarce resources to people in need. Once we agree that dignity needs validation through expressions of public respect, then we must ask: How is dignity threatened by allocation policies that restrict access by means-testing? Do we say, as some advocates do, that "means-tested programs are invariably mean?" Are there distinctive threats to dignity in old age raised by the administration and procedures of means-tested programs?

We ask these questions in despair but without any assurance of a clear answer. Exactly why is means-testing a problem, a threat to dignity? Is it a result of the residual ethic of the old Poor Laws with their focus on "blaming the victim" and attribution of personal fault? Is the problem a matter of a minimum threshold for income? For assets? Is invasion of privacy the problem? Or the bureaucratic mechanism of certifying that one falls below the threshold? Or that programs that serve poor people are just poor programs—poorly administered and without adequate protection for the least advantaged (Medicaid pays so little that providers are often reluctant to treat Medicaid patients)?[8] Or is it simply a matter of poor communication between the applicant and the eligibility worker because the process demeans both the applicant as well as the worker so that in the end, neither receives respect from the other?

PUBLIC BENEFITS ANNO 1997

Public benefits or "entitlements" refer to services or benefits, funneled through a government agency, that are distributed through administrative protocols to those who have established eligibility. Entitlement programs in the United States are not all universal. Some are "insurance-based" or "earned" and funded through prior contributions made to the program (Social Security for example). Others are based on "categorical" eligibility through membership in distinct population subgroups (half-fare cards for senior citizens, for example). Some are "means-tested" and are funded through general tax revenues (including Medicaid, Supplemental Security Income and Food Stamps).

The central similarity between all entitlements is that they are enacted into law; tend to be administered by a government agency; and, that once eligibility has been established, the benefits are considered the *property* of the beneficiary that cannot be arbitrarily removed or curtailed. The United States Supreme Court held in a landmark case in 1970 that: ". . . to cut off a welfare recipient in the face of . . . 'brutal need,' without a prior hearing of some sort is unconscionable, unless overwhelming considerations justify it."[9]

But this abstract concept of entitlements, in the end, comes up against politics: which population groups will be covered and who will be excluded? How will benefits or entitlements be distributed? How should people qualify? How will the programs be paid for? And should the poor receive the same amount, or quality of care, as the rich who pay for services out of their own pockets?

And, as we have seen in the recent debates about welfare reform, providing services through guaranteed entitlements presents another problem: *who will be served when resources are scarce*? The answers to these questions depend in part on *the public attitude towards the disadvantaged groups* that stand to benefit from the social policies–and public attitudes are changing.

The elderly in the 1960s and 1970s were considered a rather homogeneous group, suffering from frailty and ill health, experiencing a fair amount of financial hardship, and lacking adequate social supports–thereby making them imminently "deserving" of public support. In the 1980s and 1990s, on the other hand, the common perception of the elderly had changed to such a degree that elders are now considered "greedy geezers," who "are taking a free ride on the backs of other people's children."

Similarly, the Social Security program of the 1930s which was supposed to be the "harvest of a fruitful life," although still hugely popular with the general public, is now proclaimed by some quarters to be a "chain letter game" or a "pay-as-you-go Ponzi scheme" that stands to bankrupt the country. As Peter Peterson of the Concord Coalition claims: "Social Insecurity: Unless We Act Now, The Aging of America Will Become An Economic Problem That Dwarfs All Other Issues."[10]

As a result of the economic problems of the 1980s and early 1990s public entitlements, whether they are the popular "universal" programs such as Social Security and Medicare or means-tested programs such as Supplemental Security Income or Medicaid, are now being reevaluated as never before, and they are being found to be riddled with problems, although the answers to these problems remain elusive.

POVERTY, MEANS-TESTING, AND DIGNITY

In the United States access to needs-based entitlements has always been limited to those who are "truly needy" or the "deserving
poor" and need is usually defined in the American context as *financial need* and programs that address it either "screen someone in or
screen someone out of a particular program."[11] Eligibility for public benefits is assumed to be a temporary condition and poverty by
itself is not necessarily a basis for claiming entitlement (most of the
means-tested entitlements offer services to the impoverished elderly, the disabled, and families with children, leaving a large proportion of the chronically unemployed and other adult poor behind
without any public support). Eligibility for public means-tested
benefits is based on a particular set of criteria: poverty, unemployment, old age, physical frailty, disease, blindness, deafness, all of
which have some negative connotations. In order to satisfy eligibility requirements, an applicant has to overcome preliminary suspicion, cope with negative stereotyping, and often rebut a presumption
of wrongdoing or fault. The application process typically involves a
"searching inquiry" intended to prevent fraud but the process often
has an unspoken agenda of "guilty until proven innocent."[12]

The application process takes place in front of relatively low-income eligibility workers who see much poverty and hardship and
who may not show much compassion in individual cases. Their affect
is usually businesslike, curt, sometimes impatient, and always impersonal; there may even be an undercurrent of disdain for the applicants who, after all, did not adequately provide for themselves. There
may be language and communication problems and differences in
cultural or ethnic backgrounds. Welfare offices are not known for
their ability to offer privacy; most of the applications and interviews
are done in public view, among many other applicants and workers.

The personal experience of applying for a means-tested program
is profoundly unpleasant, one that easily erodes the applicant's
sense of self-worth and that, in the end, may not amount to much.
Most income programs leave recipients still below the national
poverty level of $657.50 per month for a household of one in 1997.
For instance, in New York State, which offers a supplement to the
federal SSI benefit, the maximum SSI grant for one is $556.00 per

month in 1997–although SSI eligibility does offer other important ancillary benefits such as automatic eligibility for Medicaid. But, regardless of the benefit to be obtained, the process of applying is found to be so destructive of dignity because of the way means-tested programs must be administered to comply with their public mandate, that many simply refuse to apply altogether.

This leads us to another set of questions: is the application process as demeaning for all means-tested programs or are there differences among means-tested programs? Are the benefits as minimal across the board as they may be in some of the means-tested programs? Are means-tested entitlements that are based on a need that is other than financial, different from those that are based on poverty alone? How about means-tested *health care programs* where poverty is an ancillary factor to medical need?

These are not purely rhetorical questions. For example, when establishing eligibility for Medicaid, the major means-tested health care program for the poor, the applicant must expose herself to the same conditions that cause shame in applying for income programs: having to admit to poverty and having to ask for assistance. Yet, there is a psychological difference between documenting *financial impoverishment* and *medical need*, since medical need is caused by illness, frailty, and high out-of-pocket "spenddown" of personal resources, factors that cannot be attributed to "personal fault." And, when need is defined as *medical* the erosion of dignity may be less of a personal issue, and indeed, eligibility for benefits often depends on a cost-sharing arrangement.

For example, in Medicaid coverage for nursing home care, the resident, after having spent her excess resources and turned over most of her income, obtains all other care through Medicaid. Means-testing in this context is about cost-sharing rather that "getting something for nothing" and, it can be argued, is therefore less stigmatizing for beneficiaries.

FAMILY RESPONSIBILITY
AND MEANS-TESTED PROGRAMS

As resources become more scarce, questions arise about the obligation of family members to care for elderly impoverished relatives and to what extent relatives (spouses and adult children) are morally or financially responsible for the welfare of elderly family members. Paradoxically, at this juncture, applicants and beneficiaries of public means-tested programs are adversely affected by any assistance voluntarily provided by the family. For example, when an SSI applicant receives a bag of groceries from a relative, the value of the groceries is supposed to be reported, so that the amount can be deducted from the SSI benefit, leaving the elder with less cash for the month.

Questions of family responsibility also typically arise in matters of Medicaid eligibility when an elderly person is required to "spend down" accumulated assets in order to qualify for this means-tested health care program. When a grandmother must use up assets intended for an inheritance or the support of grandchildren, in order to qualify for health care, the process of "spend down" can be experienced as demoralizing and demeaning, an assault on dignity and intergenerational solidarity. Furthermore, in the public eye, wealthy children who visit elderly parents on Medicaid in a nursing home, are viewed with suspicion and some disdain, although there is at present no legal filial responsibility statute that would require children to financially support their elders.

At the same time, the media claims that the middle class is clamoring to divest itself of assets in order to become eligible for Medicaid to obtain needed long term care services (home care or nursing home care). To what degree American families actually divest themselves of their assets for the sole purpose of becoming Medicaid eligible, is unknown; what is known, however, is that Medicare is wholly inadequate when it comes to long term care, and that private long term care insurance policies are prohibitively expensive except for the wealthy, leaving the middle class and the near-poor without adequate long term care coverage. Rather than a boondoggle for the wealthy, the Medicaid program should be considered a casualty of the lack of a social policy for long term care in the United States.

UNDERUTILIZATION OF MEANS-TESTED PROGRAMS

For years studies have shown that there is significant under-utilization of the Supplemental Security Income program (SSI) and

Medicaid. The Social Security Administration estimated in 1993 that 47% of eligible elderly are not enrolled in SSI and that about 60% of the population in poverty (of all ages) is not enrolled in the Medicaid program.[13]

When SSI was enacted in 1972, replacing various state welfare programs for the elderly poor, disabled and blind (presumably the deserving poor), it was purposefully placed under the governance of the Social Security Administration to ensure that any semblance of welfare would be minimized and to avoid stigmatization of applicants and beneficiaries. Sensitivity to the issue of dignity can also be gleaned from the fact that the program offers cash benefits (not vouchers), and does not dictate how the funds should be spent (in the way Food Stamps limit the items that can be purchased), although SSI is limited to covering "basic needs" such as clothing, food, and shelter.

Notwithstanding all good intentions, the SSI program's application process is just as burdensome to an applicant as any other means-tested program and, as noted, the program remains significantly underutilized. The public response to underutilization of SSI has been to allocate funds in recent years to conduct "outreach" to the elderly and the disabled poor with mixed result.

The Medicaid program was enacted as companion legislation to Medicare in 1965 and was designed to offer health care services for the poor who would not be covered by Medicare and who, without it, would not have any health insurance. Medicaid is funded through federal, state, and local cost-sharing mechanisms and offers a wide variety of services and programs. States have individual options to determine target populations and the extent of the services that will be offered in addition to the mandatory ones. In most states the Medicaid programs are administered by the Social Services Departments or the Departments of Public Health. Medicaid is also underutilized but the public policy response to underutilization of Medicaid has been absent and no "outreach" has been done in recent years. On the contrary, spending in the Medicaid program is considered "out of control."

Medicaid is indeed an expensive program–not because too many ineligible people benefit from it, not necessarily because of "fraud," but primarily because a very significant portion of Medicaid funds covers expensive nursing home care, needed by elderly people. It is indeed virtually the only public program that covers costly nursing home care (on average Medicare only covers from 2% to 3% of nursing home costs). As a result, Medicaid, the health insurance program for the poor, has now become a long term care program for the elderly middle class. This fact is acknowledged and supported by a recent act of Congress which enacted a law for the Prevention of Spousal Impoverishment, which addresses the plight of elderly couples when one spouse needs nursing home care. Under this federal provision the nursing home applicant can transfer up to almost $80,000 to his wife and turn over his income for her monthly support, without penalty and still obtain Medicaid-covered care. And yet, notwithstanding this important medical care program, many elders refuse to apply for Medicaid because of the stigma that associates it with "welfare." As one social work advocate recently said: ". . . My client does not want to spend down to Medicaid because she sees it as a program for people who never worked in their lives . . ."

Whether we are discussing means-tested income programs or means-tested health care programs, experience in the United States amply confirms that means-testing is experienced as demoralizing, so much so that elderly people who would be fully entitled to means-tested benefits refuse to apply for them in part because of the assault on dignity entailed by the process itself and the public's attitude towards those who depend on the government for income and health care needs.

The despair remains and we wonder, is the process of means-testing simply so demeaning, by necessity, that all sense of dignity must, in the end, be eroded? Are there other ways to ensure that the disadvantaged receive care through programs that are less damaging to self-esteem and dignity? What can we learn from other programs here in the United States or elsewhere that are funded through ways that combine public solidarity, private responsibility, and equity in the allocation of scarce resources?

PRIVATE CHARITY AND DIGNITY

Private charities often argue that their services are provided with sensitivity to the element of dignity and that the recipients of their benefits do not experience the same sense of shame that accompanies the receipt of public benefits.

Of course, there are major differences in the way charities are able to distribute benefits or obtain the resources to distribute benefits. Charities choose their beneficiaries and maintain control over the administration of the programs. Private charity can be withheld or, once given, can be withdrawn; it is not a civil right and it can violate the norms of distributive justice. In the American context, these characteristics of private charity are not understood to be deficiencies. Charitable *giving*, after all, is encouraged and may well promote solidarity (within certain limits) even if it is based on ideas different from universal citizenship or the welfare state. Charitable giving, insofar as it is linked to group solidarity, may even promote a sense of dignity. Furthermore, giving to private charity may also unconsciously be regarded as an "insurance policy against adversity" (those who give while they are financially secure, may feel they have a greater claim to receiving assistance when they are faced with adversity).

Yet, insofar as charity is never a "right" since "someone gets something for nothing," an element of uncertainty is introduced (the gift may be taken away). And if charity is based on presumptive attributes of weakness or vulnerability, it can undercut self-respect and a sense of dignity, which is why some critics have argued against charity, fearing that it demeans people, either directly or in subtle ways.

THE FUTURE OF ENTITLEMENTS IN THE UNITED STATES

Congressman Christopher Cox (R-CA), a member of the Bipartisan Commission on Entitlement and Tax Reform, established by President Clinton, commenting on all entitlements stated that the word itself has become a *"yoke around the neck of any elected official"* who tries to address it.[14] In the press, the rhetoric quickly escalated to headlines that warn us about "inter-generational warfare" brought about by "a tsunami of baby boomer retirements that is going to bust the bank."

The future direction of the public policy debate is likely to be affected by false public assumptions, a perceived inter-generational conflict, an emphasis on individual choice and personal responsibility, a growing emphasis on market forces, and policies that move away from the solidarity paradigm associated with universal programs such as Social Security and Medicare that are more compatible with maintaining dignity in old age.

"Blame is inherently antithetical to dignity and solidarity,"[15] and yet, blaming the victim is common today with "facts" put forth by lawmakers and the press that do not tell the story and that are mostly incorrect and inflammatory. For instance the *New York Post* claimed in the spring of 1997 that middle class immigrants bring their elderly parents temporarily to the United States, then: ". . . guide them through the immigration process and get them signed up for SSI. Once the checks . . . start rolling in, the scammers send the elderly immigrants home and pocket the money . . ."[16] Other common assumptions include the following:

- the elderly, the poor, and immigrants are a drain on society;
- the elderly are receiving too great a share of benefits; as a result they drive a wedge between generations;
- children are more needy and more deserving;
- the disabled (including disabled children) exaggerate their infirmities so that they can receive public benefits;
- families have stopped caring and they should be forced to take more responsibility;
- open-ended entitlements are a major cause of budget deficits;
- the federal government should get out of the entitlement business because states can do this more efficiently;
- there is a great deal of fraud committed in relation to benefits;
- entitlements foster dependence; they should be time-limited and beneficiaries should work for them; and
- the deserving poor are to be limited to American citizens.

In fact, this last exclusion leads to a broader question: are there other groups who should not be covered? In terms of both widely shared public attitudes and specific public policies, there are groups that are disfavored; these include in addition to all immigrants (recent immigrants as well as legal immigrants who have lived, worked, and paid taxes for decades in the United States), people who have abused their own bodies (alcoholics, drug abusers, perhaps people with AIDS); and people who wilfully create conditions of potential eligibility (teenage mothers and welfare mothers who give birth; disabled children who are coached to fake their disabilities; elderly who transfer assets to preserve the family fortune for their children and grandchildren; absent fathers who do not pay child support).

A major focus of Social Security reform is "privatization" in which all Americans would have "ownership" of an individual or personal security account. There are several proposals being considered at this time, all of which in some degree or other favor investment in the marketplace as the solution to Social Security's problems. And although personal choice might arguably be one way to foster "dignity," an increased emphasis on personal choice and responsibility ignores the fact that all Americans would need an adequate income in order to be able to invest in their future security adequately. Furthermore, privatization is likely to erode solidarity:

> Even partial privatization threatens to increase social divisions in the US at a time when we are already divided enough by an increasingly unequal distribution of income, by falling wages for the less well-educated, as well as by rising levels of poverty, poor public schools, and inadequate health insurance for the working poor. . . . the unspoken appeal of privatization may well be that it allows the middle class to reduce its commitment to help those who are less fortunate . . .[17]

How or whether there should be means-testing of Medicare for long-term care is another issue which will be part of the public debate although it is likely to remain unresolved as long as health care is divorced from economic security (in the public's eye, as well in the eye of lawmakers).

Several questions remain that will merit answers: Is means-testing the same as affluence-testing? Does affluence-testing affect dignity and self-esteem? Will affluence testing affect issues of solidarity?

As a general matter means-testing and affluence-testing are not identical:

... Defying years of common usage ... a new jargon has been developed, in which "means-testing" does not mean what ordinary language suggests: setting eligibility on the basis of financial need. Instead, it refers to scaling insurance premiums to income. With this novel semantic twist, 'means-testing Medicare' connects the 'undeserving poor' on welfare with the supposedly undeserving rich on Medicare. . . .[18]

Means-testing is intended to screen people in or out of a public program, by imposition of strict income limits. Affluence-testing on the other hand, is not about establishing poverty so much as it is about establishing personal cost-sharing ability; as a result, affluence testing does not affect dignity the way means-testing does. In as much as affluence-testing offers individuals an opportunity to show their wealth, it may even enhance feelings of self-worth. One of the main arguments against affluence-testing for Medicare benefits has been that enrollment by the wealthy will fall away, especially for the optional Medicare Part B program, if they are asked to pay higher out-of-pocket for services that remain fairly limited, and that might be more generously obtained elsewhere. If the wealthier and healthier segment of Medicare eligibles fall away, we run the risk that a two-tiered medical care system will develop, with different standards and quality of care for the poor and the less healthy on the one hand, and wealthy, healthy elderly on the other, or what Robert Reich calls: "the retreat of the affluent" thereby further eroding the universal aspect of the Medicare program that governed it since its inception.

In conclusion Theda Skocpol of Harvard University should have the last word:

... From early in our nation's history, successful American social policies have shared certain basic features. From public schools and Civil War benefits in the nineteenth century, through early twentieth-century programs for mothers and children, and on to Social Security, the GI Bill, and Medicare, effective and politically popular U.S. programs have all embodied a recognizable moral rationale and encompassed broad constituencies. The best American social programs have promised supports for individuals in return for service to the larger community . . . offering substantial and honorable help to retired workers who are understood to have contributed to the nation through lifetimes of work . . . Keep the health of American democracy in mind as you proceed, lest you leap too rashly into the brave new world of radically restructuring a program that most of your fellow citizens view as a keystone of the nation's social contract and a cherished support for their life story.[19]

NOTES

1. Martha Holstein; The Normative Case: Chronological Age and Public Policy. *Generations*, Vol. XIX, No. 3, Fall 1995.

2. John Dixon and Robert P. Scheurell, editors; *Social Security Programs: A Cross-Cultural Comparative Perspective*. Greenwood Press, 1995.

3. Lawrence H. Thompson; Advantages and Disadvantages of Different Social Welfare Strategies. *International Social Security Review*, Vol. 48, No. 3-4, 1995.

4. Max J. Skidmore; Social Security in the United States; in *Social Security Programs: A Cross-Cultural Comparative Perspective*. Greenwood Press, 1995.

5. Robert J. Meyers; *What Everyone Should Know About Social Security*. The Seniors Coalition, Washington DC, 1993.

6. Judith G. Gonyea; Age-Based Policies and the Oldest-Old. *Generations*, Vol. XIX, No. 3, Fall 1995.

7. AARP Public Policy Institute; *Profiles of Long-Term Care Systems Across the States*. Washington, DC, 1994.

8. Richard J. Manski, Douglas Peddicord, and David Hyman; Medicaid, Managed Care, and America's Health Safety Net. *Journal of Law, Medicine & Ethics*, 25, 1997.

9. Goldberg v. Kelly, 397 U.S. 254 (1970), which affirmed that public assistance is protected by the Fifth Amendment of the United States Constitution which states in part: ". . . nor shall any state deprive any person of life, liberty, or property without due process of law . . ."

10. Jerry L. Mashaw and Theodore R. Marmor; The Great Social Security Scare. *The American Prospect*, No. 29, November-December, 1996.

11. Elizabeth A. Kutza; Medicaid: The Shifting Place of the Old in a Needs-Based Health Program. *Generations*, Vol. XIX, No. 3, Fall 1995.

12. R. Goodin; Self-Reliance versus the Welfare State. *Journal of Social Policy*, 14: 25-47, 1985.

13. American Association of Retired Persons; Public Benefits: Who Gets Them and Who Still Needs Them? *AARP Reach*, D 15739 (2/95).

14. Bipartisan Commission on Entitlement and Tax Reform; *Final Report to the President*. Washington, DC, January 1995.

15. ibid.

16. Douglas Montero; Elderly Aliens on Dole Lie & Take It With 'em. *New York Post*, Sunday, April 20, 1997.

17. Jeff Madrick; Social Security and Its Discontents. *The New York Review of Books*, Vol. XLIII, No. 20, Dec. 19, 1996.

18. Ted Marmor and Jacob Hacker; "Means-Testing Medicare" is a Bad Idea. *Albany Times Union*, July 16, 1997.

19. Theda Skocpol; *Pundits, People, and Medicare Reform* (Conference paper). Harvard University, 1997.

Philanthropy and Government: Partners in the Community of Caring

Rose Dobrof, DSW

The root meaning of the word *philanthropy* is to be found in the Greek word philanthropia, a combination of the word for love and for man, and the dictionary definition includes reference to both the *disposition* and the *effort* to advance human welfare. Thus the emphasis is on *both* temperament and action. Here the subject is *organized philanthropy* which refers to those institutions of society–philanthropic foundations, health and social welfare groups, nonprofit associations, agencies, and organizations–which are governed and supported by individuals and families and which have as their goal the mobilization of resources to improve society and the condition of human beings in the society. Clearly both disposition and effort are necessary to the creation and sustaining of these institutions.

Organized philanthropy takes on different roles, depending, at least in part, on the political lens we adopt in viewing its activities. For conservatives, philanthropy represents a wellspring of private initiative and altruism, beginning within kinship groups, and then expanding to include neighborhood associations, community organizations, groups of like-minded people striving to find solutions to social problems. Conservatives tend to believe not only that the domain of organized philanthropy should be free of the contamination of government, but that private philanthropy is the preferred approach to ministering to the needs of people, preferred, that is, in

[Haworth co-indexing entry note]: "Philanthropy and Government: Partners in the Community of Caring." Dobrof, Rose. Co-published simultaneously in *Journal of Gerontological Social Work* (The Haworth Press, Inc.) Vol. 29, No. 2/3, 1998, pp. 147-154; and: *Dignity and Old Age* (ed: Robert Disch, Rose Dobrof, and Harry R. Moody) The Haworth Press, Inc., 1998, pp. 147-154. Single or multiple copies of this article are available for a fee from The Haworth Document Delivery Service [1-800-342-9678, 9:00 a.m. - 5:00 p.m. (EST). E-mail address: getinfo@haworthpressinc.com].

comparison to government agencies. In New York City, for example, some years ago Senior Centers which had been operated by the City Department of Social Services, were "privatized"; that is, administrative responsibility for them was transferred to the City Department for the Aging, which then contracted with voluntary agencies and churches and synagogues for the operation of the Centers. The case for this transfer of administrative and operational responsibility was made on two grounds: first, it was expected that there would be a reduction in the allocation of funds from the city budget to the centers; and, second, the claim was made that the centers would become more able to respond to the needs of older people as individuals, more effective in developing programs congruent with the cultural and ethnic values of the people in the neighborhoods in which the centers were located.

By contrast, for liberals philanthropic dollars should be used for a variety of purposes, including to support services and provisions *above* the publicly funded and sanctioned benefits to which people are *entitled* as citizens. And for liberals, the essential, core function of philanthropy is to support a seedbed for social innovation, a laboratory in which new approaches to the meeting of human needs can be developed and tested, and the successful strategies can then become part of government programs. The settlement houses, particularly in the years of the Progressive Era, provide us with a particularly vivid example of the philanthropically funded voluntary agency as laboratory for social experimentation: home care, adult education, shelters for young women alone in the city, senior centers, citizenship classes for immigrants in the neighborhood—these are among the programs which began as experimental programs in the settlement houses, and there proved their worthiness for support from tax levy dollars.

Liberals and conservatives today are together in their belief that philanthropy is part of the "independent sector"–distinct from both the government and the for-profit sectors in our society–and an essential in our striving for a civil society, one that reflects shared ideals and aspirations. The differences between liberals and conservatives are consequential, particularly in their views of the role of government and that of philanthropy, and the relationship between the two. These differences are important in our consideration of dignity in old age and in our search for ways to protect and sustain the dignity of older people in our society.

One important connection between philanthropy and aging must be noted here: households headed by a person 55 + have the highest net worth of any age group in the United States. That fact, combined with the facts that for most of these householders, the most expensive years of child rearing are over or nearing their end, and the propensity of members of this age cohort to support philanthropic causes, means that the elderly are a strategic source of money for these causes. Through gifts and bequests, older people create and sustain private philanthropy; hence, it is not surprising that philanthropic activities reflect concerns of older people, whether the goal is landmark preservation or support of cultural institutions like libraries and concert halls, or hospitals, or social service agencies.

Even given the size and influence of the philanthropic sector, the question of why private philanthropy is required at all must be attended, and particularly why private philanthropy is needed to support the ideal of dignity in old age. The answer is that in our mixed systems of education, health, and social services, some elements of dignity, some approaches to sustaining dignity in the lives of older people can probably never be programs which operate as units of government agencies. This despite the reality that the line dividing the public and voluntary sectors has never been impenetrable, that the mixing of governmental and philanthropic funds, the allocation of tax levy dollars to institutions in the philanthropic sector are not phenomena unique to modern times. Nonetheless, even if we ignore liberal or conservative assumptions about what activities properly are the province of public agencies and what are reserved to the voluntary sector, it is clear that there are some provisions which the government cannot make at all.

Even Beatrice and Sidney Webb, the leading theoreticians of the Fabian movement in England and architects of the Welfare State, nonetheless believed that the government was foreclosed from certain activities and that there remained an important role for philanthropically supported programs and services developed in "the delightful unconventionality" of the voluntary agency. These activities constitute the core, the very essence of private philanthropy, while other provisions may overlap government and philanthropic sponsorship. For example, health care or cultural institutions, support of the needy or of scientific research are all activities that can be supported either by government or private philanthropy or a combination of both.

They are not, therefore, at the core of the philanthropic sector. But at least for now, and at least in the United States, religion, along with activities reflecting personal values and meaning, can not be directly supported by government, even if their values embody essential elements of human dignity.

Let us look more closely at the several important purposes in American society served by philanthropy and voluntary organizations. In the first place, philanthropy permits us to respond to the diversity, especially ethnic and religious diversity of our society. Torres-Gil defines three forces which, he says, will shape our aging society, one of which is the increasing diversity of our nation, and of the elders among us. Our public agencies must, of course, be governed by rules of fairness and equality, but historically it has been the associations and organizations in the voluntary sector which have been most responsive to the imperatives of ethnic and religious diversity.

In the second place, philanthropy provides a vehicle for the expression of altruism in ways that government services do not. Jane Addams, founder of Hull House, wrote of "the objective necessity of the settlement house" by which she meant the social and economic problems faced by the "neighbors" of Hull House, and inevitable, she thought, in an industrialized, urban society. But she wrote also of "the subjective necessity of the settlement house," the need of educated, upper-middle-class young people, particularly women, for a vehicle to express their altruistic feelings, their sense of responsibility to the poor of the cities of the nation.

The present-day philosopher, Alan Ryan, writes of the "moral anxieties of uppermiddle-class young people like Jane Addams," who . . . "felt their lives would be meaningless if they were not devoted to 'service.'" And in our own time, philosopher-physician, Lewis Thomas, writes about "the most fundamental of all our biological necessities"–"the drive to be useful." Our search for meaning, our need to have a purpose beyond ourselves and our families are best served in a society in which there is organized philanthropy, voluntary activities which give us the opportunity to fulfill Thomas's biological necessity.

In the third place, in the United States philanthropy is inextricably linked to the evolution of mediating structures; that is, networks of churches, neighborhood groups and fraternal organizations that can mediate the distance between individuals and their families and the impersonal and large bureaucracies of government. These mediating structures are able to respond to individual and communal needs in ways that are closer to people and their families. Moreover, even when government is local–the school board, the town or county administration–it remains constitutionally constrained from seeming to favor one religious or ethnic group at the expense of another. Yet it is often a crucial ingredient of dignity in old age to insure that distinctive ways of life be maintained: Polish or Italian celebrations of holidays, the home for the aged under Jewish auspices where the laws and rituals of the religion are honored, the Black church, for generations the institutional focus of spirituality, the communal mainstay of life, and the social and educational center for its members and the community it serves.

Mediating structures, then, are not to be equated simply with the devolution of authority for funding or service provision to levels of government closer to people. Devolution may or may not be defensible in its own terms, but, in itself, it need not strengthen mediating structures nor the related values that are supportive of dignity in old age. By contrast, when philanthropy or voluntary associations take on service functions that might be performed by public agencies, or that are sub-contracted by such agencies, as in the case of the privatization of New York City's Senior Centers, these particular mediating structures do minimize the distance between government and individuals in a qualitative way.

Earlier we cited Torres-Gil's assertion that diversity is among the three primary forces affecting aging now and in the future. Beyond ethnic and religious diversity, there is an ongoing trend toward the heterogeneity of the older population in our nation and others because of the process of aging itself. Contrary to the negative stereotype of people becoming more alike as they age, it now seems clear that the developmental process of human beings is toward more individuality, more differences among us, and that this tendency probably is a function of biological or genetic differences. These biological factors are reflected in such individual differences as life expectancy, health status, and susceptibility to illness, but probably the most powerful factors associated with the heterogeneity of the older population are the social inequalities that shape individual opportunity structures over the life course itself.

One aspect of cumulative advantage or disadvantage over the life course is a tendency toward magnification of earlier life events, both positive and negative. The result is that just as children grow up to divergent positions in society, so adults age along different paths in different ways. It is far easier to predict the behavior of a "typical" 2-year old, or even 12-year old than a "typical" 80-year old, and the youngsters in the nursery school class for 3-year old's will be much more similar to each other than will be the 70-year old's in the current events discussion group at the Senior Center.

The increase in the heterogeneity of our society and the elderly within it has important implications for what it means to treat people in ways that show respect of individual differences. For example, the provision of services for residents in a long-term care facility tend to follow a rule-governed pattern, in keeping with the logic of institutional life. But a rule-governed approach, whether promoted by government, the marketplace, or a formal service system, will always tend to be unresponsive to individual differences, whether in the name of efficiency, uniformity, or justice. Regardless of good intentions or overall societal benefit, the result of a rule-governed approach may still threaten individual dignity in profound and imponderable ways. Most of the cases which Rosalie Kane and Arthur Caplan presented in their study of everyday ethics in nursing homes had to do with the need of residents to protect their individuality and dignity in a setting governed by rules and regulations in the name of efficiency and fairness.

Neither efficiency nor equality, neither the marketplace nor legal prescriptions can reach the more intangible values of dignity and individuality. And in a world of commercialization or bureaucracy, dignity is, therefore, increasingly at risk, and particularly is this so when individuals, like the aged residents of long-term care facilities, are vulnerable and largely powerless. *Au fond*, philanthropy and voluntary organizations serve as a "conscience," a voice that bears witness to, reaffirms the importance of other values too easily left out of our system of social accounting.

But even this version of the matter is incomplete, because philanthropy and voluntary organizations serve yet another purpose. They are the custodians of society's "moral capital": that is, those accumulated values and aspirations that transcend any single generation and bind us together in ties of solidarity. In the absence of such moral capital, human motivation can too easily become selfish, or perhaps outwardly ethical in a rule-governed fashion, but never full responsive to claims that reach toward a more distant past and future, aspirations that define who we are as a society, as a people, beyond a contingent collection of individuals.

Respect for elders requires some sympathy for such transcendent values, because there comes a time when the very old are "useless" to society and are protected only by a transcendent sense of obligation. That sense of obligation is perhaps best expressed in Biblical injunctions:

> Honor thy Father and thy Mother as the
> Lord thy God commanded thee, that thy
> days may be long, and that it may go
> well with thee, upon the land which
> the Lord thy God giveth thee.

or

> Cast me not out in old age . . .

or

> Rise up before the hoary head of
> the old man.

Philanthropic and voluntary organizations, whether they function under religious auspices or not, keep alive this remembrance that to be human and to be old is more than to be a collection of "needs" and "disabilities" or to be a "case" to be managed. An old person is more than "a coat upon a stick."

There is yet one more justification for philanthropic and voluntary organizations as a vehicle for the expression of altruism in our society, and now our point of vantage is older people and their need for maintenance of their roles as givers, as altruists. Rosow was one of the first to describe old age as a "roleless role," which is another way of saying that anyone who falls outside some conventional social role is at risk of being deprived of the respect that goes with performance of that role. Even accumulated wealth, prestige from past accomplishments, and other positive attributes do not necessarily compensate for loss of role. The often heard plaint of residents in long-term care facilities–"Nobody here knows who I was"–gives poignant voice to the psychological cost of the loss of role and status and identity that can be the fate of the old–in institutions and in the community as well.

When older people themselves are in giving roles, in altruistic roles, then this transposition may compensate to a degree for the loss of other roles. Erikson wrote about the need of older people for "social opportunities to experience grand-generativity," with the word grand-generativity encompassing both concern for the future and caring for those who are part of the older person's life in the present. The opportunity to experience grand-generativity–to be needed, to continue in the role of giver–Erikson said, contributes to the older person's "sense of immortality," a sense of transcendent importance in the face of the despair that many feel as the end of life comes near.

Whether the gift the older person gives is material–a contribution to a voluntary association, tuition money for the grandchild in college–or less tangible, time as a volunteer cuddling HIV+/AIDS babies in a public hospital or tutoring school age children–is in the role as giver, as altruist, as someone still connected to others that older people experience a sense of enduring meaning–Erikson's sense of immortality. Even the frail older people can give love and comfort to a troubled daughter or son or friend. It is this role of giver that can be a source of dignity for older people, and if for no other reason, this is why our society must provide opportunities for people to continue to play this role–even in the last years of their lives.

Dignity for the Oldest Old:
Can We Afford It?

Malcolm L. Johnson, PhD

Dignity for the oldest old–can we afford it? Before I left Bristol for New York I said goodbye to Tom, a man I have known for 30 years, a likeable, modest man, who has always worked hard and cared greatly for his family. A gunner in the Second World War he hardly ever mentioned those 5 years out of his life when he was doing something else, being somewhere else, fighting for his country. Instead, after all that, he raised chickens to supplement his income from his day job so that his daughter could have a university education. In those days he was a man of sinewy strength and practical competence. When I left him yesterday he was living in the garden flat of our Victorian house in Bristol to which we all moved six weeks ago. Aged almost 85, he suffers form multi-infarct dementia, he is doubly incontinent, he is virtually blind, he can hardly hear and he has suffered for a long time from diabetes. In the last 9 months he has lost the ability to control his body and cannot wash himself, cannot shave, cannot dress himself–cannot even contribute to those actions.

His wife and his daughter, with my help, are his carers. Because his care is 24 hours a day, 7 days a week, we are supported by a range of professionals and volunteers, a primary care physician, a home nurse, a bathing attendant, a community psychiatric nurse and every 3 months he goes for a week into respite care. His wife Kate

[Haworth co-indexing entry note]: "Dignity for the Oldest Old: Can We Afford It?" Johnson, Malcolm L. Co-published simultaneously in *Journal of Gerontological Social Work* (The Haworth Press, Inc.) Vol. 29, No. 2/3, 1998, pp. 155-168; and: *Dignity and Old Age* (ed: Robert Disch, Rose Dobrof, and Harry R. Moody) The Haworth Press, Inc., 1998, pp. 155-168. Single or multiple copies of this article are available for a fee from The Haworth Document Delivery Service [1-800-342-9678, 9:00 a.m. - 5:00 p.m. (EST). E-mail address: getinfo@haworthpressinc.com].

155

in nearly 84. She nursed her own father for seven years before he died, a cantankerous old preacher farmer. For 25 years she has suffered from severe depression and although caring for kin has been her life-times work, her unmarried, rather unworldly sheep farmer brother lived with them for 25 years, she now finds all of life overwhelming. Most days they both say that they will kill themselves but as the summer begins to show its face and the disruption of the house move is replaced by new routines, they say it less often.

Without their daughter's love, her care and support, they could not survive. Like many others whose children cannot, or will not support them, they would be in an old people's home. Last week Tom took himself off for an impromptu walk in a city he doesn't know. He took his walk because Kate had shouted at him and said she would kill him, he had wet his bed in the night and had soaked two sets of clothes before lunch time, and all this despite incontinence aids. After a search of the nearby streets I found him wandering along with his stick and his cap on–I found him and said what are you doing, he said Oh I am going out to bring in the sheep. I got my car. He got in the car. We drove back home, nothing was said. He had no idea what chaos he had caused, he did not know that he was lost.

This is the kind of old age that we are addressing today. That last section of life, the fourth age, the age of dependency. Tom of course is my father-in-law, and we his family the only people he remembers. Together we hold together the last vestiges of his life. He knows that we care for him and like the gentle man he always was he still smiles and says thank you and means it. That's one thing that he knows, that people are preserving his dignity and that he wants to say thank you. Is this traditional rather familiar reciprocity now a rare commodity? Has the changing family made such arrangements virtually impossible? Who can offer to provide dignity at home for those who are old and frail–indeed as a society can we afford it?

My task is to ask those questions–not just as a citizen but as a gerontologist and a policy analyst. I have 3 questions: first to examine the changing context of old age and the policy dilemmas it has created. Secondly, to consider how we can assess what we do for frail, elderly people and thirdly to explore the service delivery issues.

But first another reference to a piece of imagery. In her novel *The Children of Men*, P. D. James presents a vision of the near future where human infertility has spread like a plague–it is the year 2021–no babies have been born for a quarter of a century anywhere in the world. Very old people are being driven to despair and suicide and the final generation of young people are beautiful but violent and cruel. In amongst the mixture of tyrannical government and generational hostility the middle aged maintain a continued sense of studied normality. James offers us a moral story, a parable about how aging societies could go wildly wrong–to put the situation in stark relief she presents a world in which the young are a scarce and diminishing minority. Arrogantly aware of their elite position, they exploit their economic and social advantage at the cost of those who are old and weak and poor. Indeed it is the official policy in this mythical country of the ruling council that dependent elderly people should actually take their own lives and to promote this "socially responsible" approach the government has sponsored a method of mass suicide in which old people dressed in white are herded on to barge-like ships. Accompanied by a brass band and their own mournful singing they are taken out to sea and the ships are sunk. All on board, not very gracefully, die. In return for electing to take part in this bizarre death ritual known as the "quietus," the government rewards their relatives ironically with a pension.

This fictional representation of our world is one we recognise. It is about intergenerational competition and tension and some of that is real and some of it most certainly is not. But we should remember that the great corpus of anthropological study of old age, tells us that death hastening is a very common practice in traditional societies. We indulge in it, we both prolong life, often far too long and at the same time we hasten it–not the same people–and this is a curious paradox that we need to address under this heading of dignity.

For the first 15 years of my life as a gerontologist I struggled with politicians and policy makers to get them to understand the massive importance of the greatest change in contemporary society, that of the demographic revolution, in which for the first time in human history we would have properly balanced populations where people would expect to live their full lifespan. The challenge was to persuade them this was not some kind of post war bulge, this was not the product of men who had been away for 4 or 5 years and were exercising their youthful lust, this is for good, this is permanent, this is the way society *will be* (unless there is some awful eventuality) forever–this is the new structure of the population. They did not listen. Politicians do not want to hear something which is more than three years ahead because it is not their responsibility, especially if it costs money. Those arguments were eventually heard. When they were heard and understood, the political response was panic. It was not thoughtful, it was not evaluative, it was not analytic and it had no time perspective–it was sheer panic that if this is for real, if pensions are going to rise, if social security budgets are going to go up, if elderly people consume more than half of the health care budget, though they represent less than 20% of the total population, then what we have to do is cut.

The more forward thinking politicians were genuinely exercised by the scale of the issues raised and tried hard to place the new old age on the agenda. More money and skilled person power was put into health and social services. Special housing took a higher prominence. In America the gathered might of the 30 million members of the American Association of Retired Persons along with the feisty interventions of Maggie Kuhn and her Gray Panthers created what Henry Pratt (1976) called "the Gray Lobby." In Europe older people's organisations have had less impact, not least because they presented no electoral threat. But as the recognition of a permanently changed world population structure dawned on those who make public policy, fortuitously the world economy went into decline. In the uncertainty about how to behave, two kinds of reaction emerged: one operational and the other rhetorical. The rhetoric declared a continuing commitment to older people (especially the very old), but one which had to be managed down because the financial and caring burden would be unmanageably great. Unrefined extrapolations of steeply rising pensions, housing, health and social care costs produced by actuaries and statisticians, fuelled a sense of political panic.

Observing the consequences for national exchequers and therefore for taxation levels, a new vocabulary of individual responsibility grew in resonance with political shifts to the right.

Within a remarkably short space of time, it became one kind of received political wisdom that making your own provisions for health care costs and for income in later life was a freedom.

In practice it meant two things–privatisation of public services and cost-cutting. To bolster the logic we were told that the collectivism of state welfare undetermined personal initiative. In its place we needed free market disciplines, entrepreneurship and the cost efficiency which results from competition.

It was not only the pressure from a developing global capital market wanting tighter control of national budget deficits, which militated against the variety of welfare states in Europe. As Esping Andersen's (1990) penetrating analysis revealed, the social class, labour market and public-private balance had so markedly changed in the post World War II period that existing welfare regimes had less popular support both from those who had paid for them–the growing middle class–and those who were the recipients of non-employment benefits. He argues persuasively that the growing middle class (which resulted from increased education and changes towards a post-industrial economy) was well disposed to the market model. Their disposable income was potentially increased and they were provided with more choice in ensuring the well-being of their own families.

Class factors are important variables in the shift of attitudes, but so too are greater and more successful participation by women in paid employment and the success of a layer of ethnic minority people in education and work based income. It is too simplistic to suggest, as some commentators have, that the overwhelming threat to retired populations is market economics.

We shall return to these other variables and the role they play. Nonetheless the rapid impact of New Right thinking on services and income to the old was substantial. Restraints have been placed on state pension levels; encouragement to join private pensions schemes have massively expanded the personal financial service sector, and direct services have both been out-sourced and reduced. What began as a localised infection became an international epidemic. Demographically induced gerontophobia began to manifest itself on an inter-continental scale. In most of the countries in Europe 50% or more of hospital beds were occupied by elderly people in addition to the 5-9% of the retired population resident in long stay accommodation Maltby (Walker and 1997).

To address the need to reduce expenditure, community care policies were introduced. The twin benefits of care at home where older people preferred to be, along with a presumed cost-effectiveness, drove a policy which few countries resisted. A late entrant, Canada, in its statement *Future Directions in Continuing Care* (1992) expressed the policy thrust with great clarity.

> . . . community based care should be the service of first option where appropriate: public and professional attitudes consistent with this should be fostered" and goes on to say "Continuing care should be to supplement or support, not replace, family and community caregiving."

Then the economic imperative follows:

> Continuing care services should be developed to support the lowest cost alternative appropriate to the needs of the individual.

In Europe the evidence for economic rationing of care services is unequivocal. The European Commission Observatory Report (1993) draws attention to the commonality of European policy concerns. It indicates there are 5 main issues:

- To contain the heavy growth of health expenditure
- To define policy priorities for the rapidly growing group of elderly persons
- To provide adequate coverage for the growing need for long-term care
- To re-organise long-term care
- To introduce new incentives for the development of community care and informal care.

Overall community based services–which go almost exclusively to the oldest old–across Europe have grown over the past decade, particularly in Denmark, Greece and Germany. But in Belgium the policy of blocked budgets has seen provision reduced. In Britain the number of home helps fell 30% between 1976 and 1988. (Johnson, 1994). Similarly, in the Irish Republic, the reduction in long stay beds was not matched by the expansion of community care. The report from Italy stresses that about 15% of elderly people need home care but only about 1% receive it.

In New Zealand a further episode of cost cutting followed dramatic across the board cuts in a whole range of public services and social security benefits. Remarkably, the example of decimating welfare budgets provided by this small country with a population the size of Madrid, which managed its affairs so badly it was virtually bankrupt, became a model to be admired and reproduced by previously mature nations. Such a willingness to implement untested, unevaluated policies because of their potential to reduce the call on the middle class taxpayer should disturb us all as citizens as well as in our role of gerontologists.

These twists and turns in public policy designed to achieve cost reduction now represent a set of dilemmas in all developed societies. We can see in the literature a series of shifts in the principal life domains of family; work; health; well-being and housing; and income.

To take the last first, we have seen concerted attempts to curtail and reduce expenditure on social security payments and pensions. It must be acknowledged that in this century there have been significant improvements in the financial position of retired people. But researchers still report unacceptable levels of old age poverty (Midwinter, 1997). As on so many other dimensions of old age provision, the Netherlands has low levels of official poverty with 17% below the poverty line. But in Portugal and Spain, Perista (1992) estimates the proportion is over 50%; in Britain, Walker estimates 28%; whilst pensioners in France and Germany can be described in Alber's (1993) words as "living in relative affluence rather than in relative poverty."

Whether the reaction is placed within the overtly inter-generational contest represented by the middle-aged, middle class American pressure group, Americans for Generational Equity, or in the framework of Esping Andersen's class/structural arguments, a hiatus can be observed in the willingness to further improve the financial lot of older people. Combined with the marked shift away from state to private pension it is possible to detect a re-formulation of the bond between generations (Johnson, 1995) which now requires further examination.

NEW PATTERNS OF RETIREMENT

The analysis so far has raised many issues concerning the oldest old, both for the political economy agenda and for public policy. But there is one central issue which has ramifications for all of the others–retirement.

Retirement from regular paid employment can be traced back in Europe to the middle of the nineteenth century when civil servants were eligible to retire on a small pension. It was not until later in the century when Bismarck introduced a national system in Germany that the currently recognisable system began to appear. Bismarck chose the age of 70 because by that stage most workers were genuinely old and unable or becoming unable to work. Today the average expectation of life in Northern Europe for men is about 68 and women about 72. A hundred years ago it was more than ten years less and fewer than 4% of the population lived beyond age 65 (today that figure is about 17%–it will reach 20% by about 2020).

So retirement was originally designed only for employed men, in selected occupations and with minimal financial support. Moreover, it was both the expectation and the reality that the vast majority lived for only a short time and in poor health.

Most workers carried out manual tasks in unhygienic and unsafe work places, so that over a work life of over 50 years they became progressively more sick. Those who survived to 65 were likely to be exhausted. Young and Schuller (1991) put it graphically in their book *Life After Work* when they say:

> Retirement was a kind of postscript to work which only had to be defined negatively. The watch or clock that employers traditionally handed over to their retiring workers was a deceit. It symbolised the gift of the time that was now to be their own

rather than the employers! But the new owner was going to wear out long before the watch.

So throughout human history, until recent times almost everyone worked either until they died or until they were physically incapable of going on. Life after work was only for a few survivors and for them it was an antechamber to death.

When the Old Age Pensions Act was introduced in Britain in 1908, the age of 65 was adopted–as it was in most countries of Europe, though a few delayed until age 70. Again it was only selected occupations and only for men. In the inter-war years the retirement concept extended across the developed world eventually embracing all occupations and abandoning the exclusion of women.

The post Second World War era of welfare states exemplified by those in Scandinavia and Britain made retirement and adequate state pensions available to almost everyone. Yet in this early post war period, elderly women were still seen in black clothing, virtually excluded from social life and treated as invalids. Indeed retirement, old age and dependency became virtually synonymous both in the public mind and in public policy.

As an evangelist for the full citizenship of old people, I am now acutely aware that the contemporary patterns of retirement–beneficial as they are–are unsustainable in their present forms. More to the point, the life of extended leisure presently experienced by growing numbers of retirees in not what was ever meant in earlier conceptions of intergenerational support to the old. Such a contract must rest upon a principled reinterpretation of what is equitable and what is deliverable.

There should be no doubt whatever that the rich nations of Europe and North America can more than adequately provide for all their citizens of all ages. They will have to open closed and buttressed doors like those of the immensely wealthy pension funds and re-examine inheritance practices, to release more of our collective assets. But developed nations can–and will–sustain the whole population without damaging the well-being of the young and middle aged.

The essential elements of the present system of basic state pensions and largely free health care can be funded so long as there is a

constraining realism about the limits of the rights and the responsibilities which are integral to the contract. In health care it will be
necessary to adopt more sensible, but socially sanctioned, rationing
on the basis of the probability of real health gain and for doctors to
share the treatment functions with other health practitioners. Such
practices might build on the analysis–if not the conclusions–of Dan-
iel Callaghan (1987). As for retirement as we have come to know it
over the past two decades–it will have to be radically re-assessed.
Developed societies cannot afford to forego the direct contribution of
so large a segment of their adult populations. Between two and three
decades of living outside of the mainstream of economic life is a
breach of the contract. The commitment younger generations have
inherited is to support those who cannot support themselves, not to
provide an ever growing sabbatical in the third age.

By the same token, third age people will not tolerate exclusion
from full citizenship. Nor will many of them be willing or able to
exist economically on fixed and diminishing incomes.

The capacity to continue to earn income will become an imperative for many young old, both for current living and the avoidance
of a penurious late life. So in re-thinking the generational contract it
is essential that there is a reliable platform of services and pension
provision for all. But the post-60 phase of life will need to be
greatly more flexible in offering:

- Flexible retirement between 55 and 75
- New opportunities for job changes in mid and late career–
  possibly to lower paying jobs, but ones which can go on much
  later, e.g., in the service sectors of industry and in the expanding realms of social and health care.
- The care of the old old is increasingly the responsibility of
  over 55's. Mechanisms need to be found to include some of
  this in the formal economy.
- New generations must–as in earlier times–make provision for
  their own old age through a lifetime investment. I say this
  knowing all too well that there are structural inequalities
  which will make this difficult or impossible for some. It is
  properly within the Contract for just and non-stigmatising provision to be made for them.

These proposals demand more justification and elaboration than can be provided within the confines of this paper. However, some more developed rationale is necessary for the key points about flexible retirement and the extension of remunerated employment well beyond current retirement ages. At one level the notion is one of simple practicality. If societies are unable or unwilling to make adequate financial provision for the growing population of older people, those individuals must make greater provision for themselves. There are only three broad ways in which this can be done:

i. Greater lifetime investment in savings, investments and private pensions;
ii. Increased intra-family transfers to the old;
iii. Continued earnings from employment or business activities.

The post second world war trend has already produced major increases in the capital assets (notably in owner-occupied housing) and occupational private pension provision of current pensioners. (Dahrendorf, 1995). Yet as Taverne (1995) and Townsend and Walker (1995) warn, these provisions alone will not enable substantial segments of future generations of retirees to maintain adequate income.

It can be safely predicted that at least half of current pensioners across Europe have enough financial provision to maintain themselves above accepted poverty standards and meet the costs of any long term care they need to pay for. Across the European Union countries the evidence suggests that this proportion of self-sustaining pensioners will increase modestly. But there will be a group of around one third who will either run out of savings or face major care costs beyond state provision, for which they cannot pay.

It is inevitable that the practices of the past 25 years of enforcing early retirement will create a cohort of impoverished older people, who may have up to 40 years of living without earned income. Such a group will present a mixture of financial, social, health and psychological pathologies which will wholly negate the "savings" made by their enforced exit from the work force. Both these individuals and the many others with little or no old age provision (notably those who have run modest small businesses) will find it imperative to earn money from economic activity.

In his volume, *The End of Work*, Jeremy Rifkin (1995) argues that computerisation and automation will diminish the need for labour altogether, producing even higher levels of unemployment. But his focus is only on the industrial, manufacturing and commercial sector of the formal economy. What he ignores is the growing need for human services, not least for the very old. However there will need to be even greater development of such services as some parts of family care–currently unpaid–become commodified. The evidence for continued commitment by families to supporting all those who are sick, vulnerable or disabled remains strong throughout the developed world (Kosberg, 1992; Wellman, 1989, 1992). Even cohort studies which encompass multiple generations with extensive marital breakdown reveal sustained intergenerational support (Bengtson and Harootyan, 1994). Nonetheless, the twin pressures of family over-commitment and the need of older individuals to earn money will induce the creation of a new market in home based "in situ" care which will provide one medium for the young old to increase their personal incomes.

Caring services for the very old will not be the only area of unremunerated activity to move into the economic sphere. Child care, leisure, domestic work, counselling and other non-medical therapies could all provide opportunities for those who wish to or must have gainful work beyond 65.

Contemporary thinking about employment and labour markets takes the view that opportunities for paid employment will diminish and this alone invalidates any claim by older people to remain longer in the workforce. Yet if Charles Handy (1985) is right about the changing patterns of work there will be a greater diversity of jobs and more possibility for older workers to take up part-time work on a flexible basis. Certainly, the transformation of unpaid tasks into remunerated work and the inclusion of more people in the paid economy will be on the international agenda. One increasing driving force will be the pressure from people in the 55 to 75 age band to avoid alienation and poverty.

CONCLUSIONS

Despite governmental panics the contract between the generations is not broken (Johnson, 1995; Moody, 1992; Laslett and Fishkin, 1992) but societies need to reaffirm it. The excess of individualism which has infected the world is not going to serve our collective purposes. Secondly, we can afford dignity for the oldest old because we must–and of course we will–in thirty or forty years time we will be doing it by whatever means we can't predict–but we will be doing it because it will be inconceivable that we can have the quietus and because the resources exist–we can use them better if we think more carefully with older people and listen to them. That is an economically viable proposition and not simply a bit of emotionally wished filling. And thirdly, the middle classes must see it in their interest–to contribute more of our collective wealth to the services of older people. It will be the ultimate test of developed societies in the twenty-first century, that they provide dignity for the oldest old.

REFERENCES

Alber, J. (1993). Health and Social Services. In Walker et al. *Older People in Europe: Social and Economic Policies*–Report of the European Observatory. Brussels: Commission of the European Communities.

Bengtson, V.L. and Harootyan, R.A. (eds.) (1994). *Intergenerational Linkages: Hidden Connections in American Society*. New York: Springer.

Callaghan, D. (1987). *Setting Limits: Medical Goals in an Aging Society*. Simon & Schuster: New York.

Dahrendorf, R., Field, F. et al. (1995). *Wealth Creation and Social Cohesion in a Free Society*, London: Committee on Wealth Creation and Social Cohesion.

Esping-Andersen, A.G. (1990). *The Three Worlds of Welfare Capitalism*. Cambridge: Policy Press.

Handy, C. (1985). *The Future of Work: A Guide to a Changing Society*. Oxford: Basil Blackwell.

Health and Welfare Canada. (1992). *Future Directions in Continuing Care*. Report of the Federal/Provincial/Territorial Sub-Committee on Continuing Care, Health Services and Promotion Branch, Ottawa.

Johnson, M.L. (1994). Services for Elderly People in Great Britain. In Kosberg, J.I. (ed.), *International Handbook on Services for the Elderly*. Westport: Greenwood Publishing Group.

Johnson, M.L. (1995). Interdependency and the Generational Compact. *Ageing and Society*, 15, pp. 243-265.

Kosberg, J. (ed.). (1992). *Family Care of the Elderly: Social and Cultural Changes*. Newbury Park: Sage.

Midwinter, E. (1997). *Pensioned Off: Retirement and Income Examined*. Buckingham: Open University Press.

Moody, H.R. (1992). *Ethics in an Aging Society*. Baltimore and London: Johns Hopkins University Press.

Perista, H. (1992). *Social and Economic Policies and Older People in Portugal*. Lisbon: GEGIS.

Pratt, H.J. (1976). *The Politics of Old Age*. Chicago: University of Chicago Press.

Rifkin, J. (1976). *The End of Work: The Decline of the Global Workforce and the Dawn of the Post-Market Era*. New York: Tarcher/Putnam.

Taverne, D. (1995). *The Pensions Time-Bomb in Europe*. London: Federal Trust for Education and Research.

Townsend, P. and Walker, A. (1995). *The Future of Pensions: Revitalising National Insurance*. Discussion Paper 22. London: The Fabian Society.

Walker, A; Alber, J. and Guillemard, A.M. (1993). *Older People in Europe: Social and Economic Policies*. The 1993 Report of the European Observatory, Commission of the European Communities, DGV, Brussels.

Walker, A. and Maltby, T. (1997). *Ageing Europe*. Buckingham: Open University Press.

Wellman, B. and W. Scott (1989). Brothers Keepers: Situating Kinship Relations in Broader Networks of Social Support. *Sociological Perspectives* 32, 3, Fall 1989, pp. 273-306.

Wellman, B. (1992). Which Types of Ties and Networks Provide What Kinds of Social Support? *Advances in Group Processes*, 9, pp. 207-235.

Young, M. and Schuller, T. (1991). *Life After Work: The Arrival of the Ageless Society*. London: HarperCollins.

About the Authors

Sia Arnason, MSW, is Co-Director of the Institute on Law and Rights of Older Adults of the Brookdale Center on Aging of Hunter College. She is the co-author of *The Legal Rights of the Elderly*, the *New York State Elder Law Handbook*, and other publications on rights and entitlements of the aging.

Robert Coles, MD, Professor of Psychiatry at Harvard Medical School, is the Pulitzer Prize-winning author of the nationally acclaimed *Children of Crisis* series and, more recently, *The Spiritual Life of Children* and *The Moral Life of Children*.

Jo Ann Damron-Rodriguez, PhD, is on the faculty of the School of Social Welfare at the University of California at Los Angeles, where she is an affiliate of the Geriatric Education Center. She is an authority on ethnicity and aging.

Robert Disch, MA, is Director of Intergenerational and Older Adult Education Programs at the Brookdale Center on Aging of Hunter College. He has taught literature at the Pratt Institute and in the City University of New York and is the author or editor of seven books on contemporary social issues.

Rose Dobrof, DSW, is Founding Director of the Brookdale Center on Aging and Emerita Professor, Brookdale Professor at Hunter College of Gerontology, New York. A nationally known authority in the field of aging, she is the editor of the *Journal of Gerontological Social Work* and Co-Chair of the U.S. Committee for the Celebration of the United Nations Year of the Older Person.

Linda K. George, PhD, is a sociologist who has specialized in the study of social-psychological processes linked to role change and lifespan development. A former President of the Gerontological Society of America, she has been co-editor of the *Handbook on Aging and the Social Sciences* and is the author of numerous publications in the field of gerontology.

169

Malcolm L. Johnson, PhD, was founding Editor of the journal *Ageing and Society* and former Dean of the School of Social Welfare of the Open University. He is currently Professor and Director of the School for Policy Studies at the University of Bristol.

Harry R. Moody, PhD, is Executive Director of the Brookdale Center on Aging of Hunter College, where he also teaches gerontology, philosophy, and bioethics. A philosopher by background, he is the author of *The Five Stages of the Soul* (Doubleday, 1997).

Henry C. Simmons, PhD, is Professor of Religion and Aging and Director of the Center on Aging at the Presbyterian School of Christian Education in Richmond, VA. He is the author of many articles and books on spiritual development over the lifespan.

Index

Haworth
DOCUMENT DELIVERY
SERVICE

This valuable service provides a single-article order form for any article from a Haworth journal.

- *Time Saving:* No running around from library to library to find a specific article.
- *Cost Effective:* All costs are kept down to a minimum.
- *Fast Delivery:* Choose from several options, including same-day FAX.
- *No Copyright Hassles:* You will be supplied by the original publisher.
- *Easy Payment:* Choose from several easy payment methods.

Open Accounts Welcome for . . .
- Library Interlibrary Loan Departments
- Library Network/Consortia Wishing to Provide Single-Article Services
- Indexing/Abstracting Services with Single Article Provision Services
- Document Provision Brokers and Freelance Information Service Providers

---

MAIL or *FAX* THIS ENTIRE ORDER FORM TO:

Haworth Document Delivery Service
The Haworth Press, Inc.
10 Alice Street
Binghamton, NY 13904-1580

or FAX: 1-800-895-0582
or CALL: 1-800-429-6784
9am-5pm EST

PLEASE SEND ME PHOTOCOPIES OF THE FOLLOWING SINGLE ARTICLES:
1) Journal Title: _____
   Vol/Issue/Year:_____Starting & Ending Pages:_____
Article Title:_____

2) Journal Title: _____
   Vol/Issue/Year:_____Starting & Ending Pages:_____
Article Title:_____

3) Journal Title: _____
   Vol/Issue/Year:_____Starting & Ending Pages:_____
Article Title:_____

4) Journal Title: _____
   Vol/Issue/Year:_____Starting & Ending Pages:_____
Article Title:_____

(See other side for Costs and Payment Information)

COSTS: Please figure your cost to order quality copies of an article.

1. Set-up charge per article: $8.00
   ($8.00 × number of separate articles) _____

2. Photocopying charge for each article:

   1-10 pages: $1.00 _____

   11-19 pages: $3.00 _____

   20-29 pages: $5.00 _____

   30+ pages: $2.00/10 pages _____

3. Flexicover (optional): $2.00/article _____

4. Postage & Handling: US: $1.00 for the first article/

   $.50 each additional article _____

   Federal Express: $25.00 _____

   Outside US: $2.00 for first article/
   $.50 each additional article _____

5. Same-day FAX service: $.50 per page _____

   GRAND TOTAL: _____

METHOD OF PAYMENT: (please check one)

❑ Check enclosed   ❑ Please ship and bill. PO # _____
   (sorry we can ship and bill to bookstores only! All others must pre-pay)

❑ Charge to my credit card: ❑ Visa;   ❑ MasterCard;   ❑ Discover;
   ❑ American Express;

Account Number:_____ Expiration date:_____

Signature: **X** _____

Name: _____ Institution: _____

Address: _____

_____

City: _____ State:_____ Zip:_____

Phone Number: _____ FAX Number: _____

MAIL or *FAX* THIS ENTIRE ORDER FORM TO:

Haworth Document Delivery Service	**or FAX:** 1-800-895-0582
The Haworth Press, Inc.	**or CALL:** 1-800-429-6784
10 Alice Street	(9am-5pm EST)
Binghamton, NY 13904-1580	